Baseball Monologues

Baseball Monologues

Edited by Lavonne Mueller

With an introduction by Lee Blessing

HEINEMANN
Portsmouth, NH

Heinemann
A division of Reed Elsevier Inc.
361 Hanover Street, Portsmouth, NH 03801-3912

Offices and agents throughout the world

"Elegy for the House That Ruth Built, and the Game That He Knew,"
by Arthur Kopit, and "Ted Williams," by Howard Korder, were originally presented as part of *Hitting for the Cycle,* produced by Bay
Package Productions.

Performance rights information can be found at the end of this book.

Library of Congress Cataloging-in-Publication Data
Baseball monologues / edited by Lavonne Mueller ; with an
    introduction by Lee Blessing.
        p. cm.
    ISBN 0-435-07021-5
    1. Baseball—Anecdotes. 2. Baseball—History. I. Mueller,
Lavonne.
GV873.B26 1996
796.357–dc20   96-14325
                                                              CIP

Editor: Lisa A. Barnett
Production: Vicki Kasabian
Cover design: Jenny Jensen Greenleaf
Book design: Tom Allen, Pear Graphic Design
Manufacturing: Louise Richardson

Printed in the United States of America on acid-free paper
99 98 97 96   DA   1 2 3 4 5

Contents

Introduction

LEE BLESSING

The marketing mavens behind the multimillion-dollar indus-
try that is major league baseball have recently been pushing
the button marked "nostalgia" as hard and often as they can.
Old-timers games abound, vintage uniforms crop up for
almost any special occasion and, most significant, the newest
wave of baseball stadia—Camden Yards, Jacobs Field, Coors
Field, and The Ballpark—are no longer stadia in the most
modern sense at all, but deliberate throwbacks to pre–World
War II designs.

Why such a commitment to the old-fashioned in baseball
when other major league sports are for the most part struggling to look and sound more like technospectaculars from
the next century? One reason may be that in a curious way,
baseball alone among major team sports seems to go both
forward and backward in time. No new star can shine for
long before he's compared to someone ten, twenty—even a
hundred—years ago. No statistic is too old to have deep reso-
nance for us. No one forgets that the sports equivalent of the
Civil War was fought primarily in baseball—and is there any
story in or out of sports for which we remember 1947 more
than for Jackie Robinson?

Poets, novelists, and essayists have long exploited this
quality of the game—its effortless ability to carry us anywhere in the country, anywhere in the century, at the mere
mention of a name. Tris Speaker, Roberto Clemente, Christy
Mathewson, Maury Wills, Pete Rose, Ty Cobb—each of
these names, or any of a thousand others, can take us instant-
ly on an archetypal journey of promise, endurance, triumph,
and the inevitable fall from the grace of excellence. Each of
these names still evokes a city and an era that is both gone

and with us still. We drive to games down streets that once bore trolleys full of fans to ballfields that had only wooden fences—and before that, no fences at all. In some parks a lucky few of us can sit and watch the same game our great-grandfathers watched, in their suits and ties and straw boaters, on hot July afternoons.

Little wonder that from time to time dramatists have also looked to baseball for the kinds of stories that compel us to examine our capacities—physical, mental, moral, and spiritual. As with other fields of human endeavor, the sport has been used as a context for tragedy, comedy, farce, experimental theater—even a classic Broadway musical. But always it remains quintessentially American: vibrant, hopeful, sentimental, and self-deceiving. August Wilson's *Fences,* one of the most honored plays in American history, uses baseball as its central symbol.

Major league baseball came to my hometown of Minneapolis when I was eleven. We'd almost gotten the Giants, but had to settle for the Senators—a proud, sixty-year tradition of Walter Johnson and not much else. The team name was immediately changed to the eternally hopeless Twins. Still I remember with an almost eerie clarity—and a peculiar selectiveness—the first game I went to. Jim Kaat pitched, Earl Battey hit two home runs in the 2–0 home victory, and I spent the whole game in the bottom row of the right-field bleachers staring at the back of Al Kaline—who was poised on every pitch, coiled and ready. Certainly he made plays during the game, but I don't remember any. What I do remember is the crouch, the intensity, the solitude. There, in the enormity of the brilliant green outfield under overarching night, a mystical geometry somehow connected Kaline to his distant teammates and the game itself. I had the worst seat in the house—home plate so far away it was nearly obscured by the curvature of the Earth. But I didn't need to see home. Kaline's stance alone—the careful shifting of weight from toe to toe, the last-second half-step in one direction or another—this was the game: the complete embodiment of a world I had never before seen up close. After thirty-five years I still remember the type-style of the black numeral on his back—and that it was a six.

The persistence of this memory, and of others (I once spent a wonderful evening watching a 1–0 game in which the only run scored was in the first inning—before I arrived), leads me to think that for millions of us there is a pleasure intrinsic to the game that has nothing to do with winning or losing. To watch Babe Ruth hit a towering home run or a towering pop fly was still to watch Babe Ruth, and whether one was seeing him tread majestically on home plate or kick first base in disgust while the infield fly rule was being invoked, one was still unarguably there. I never saw Ruth, of course, but I was there when Rod Carew stole home off Gaylord Perry in the year Carew matched Ty Cobb's decades-old record for steals of home. And I was there when Carew came up the next inning and Perry drilled him with the first pitch.

In Hackensack, New Jersey, just a few miles south of where baseball was invented in the parkland known as Elysian Fields, there's a small baseball diamond that sits directly atop the western entrance to the Lincoln Tunnel. I notice it each time I ride into Manhattan from Newark Airport. As the bus spirals down the wide oval of the approach ramp, it circles this field, then continues into the city where baseball was originally called "The New York Game." I've never seen a game played on this field (it look as though foul balls must bounce down onto unsuspecting cars emerging from under the Hudson), but something about its location reminds me of scrub pines growing out of sheer rock walls. A thing of subtle joys insisting on its right to exist almost anywhere.

And of course they do. Small parks and large, with and without grandstands or lights—faithful homes for the Miesville Mudhens, the Pekin Celestials, the Nazareth

Cement Dusters, and the Longview Cannibals. Birthplaces of the great players of tomorrow and tender burial ground of the dreams of everyone else. Wherever we are in America, we know a ballfield is close by; we know someone is playing catch, hitting a few fly balls, and entertaining outrageous delusions of grandeur. And we know that somewhere on one of those fields the next Hank Aaron is taking his first at-bat.

Dramatists are drawn to baseball because it's so nakedly a world in which performance is everything. And performance is measured in infinite detail. A legion of statistics attach themselves inescapably to each player: wins, losses, hits, strikeouts, steals. If a player performs at the level of a star, nothing else matters—not even his name. In baseball we speak respectfully, even reverently, of men called Wee Willie, Arky, Bobo, Wahoo, Little Poison, Nellie, Junior, and Rabbit. As a culture we ache to judge and be judged on merit alone, but few of us are strong enough to live by that principle. In baseball, there's no choice: if you can't hit the curve low and away, you're gone. If you can't turn the double play with a runner rolling into your knees, you're gone. If you can't throw heat anymore, you're gone with a vengeance. Those of us who got picked last on the softball field can at least take comfort in the fact that our livelihood doesn't depend on our continued ability to barehand a bunt on the dead run.

    Another aspect of baseball that attracts dramatists is its mimicry of the arc of a human life. In the span of some twenty years a ballplayer goes from birth to death, so to speak. Injury, alcoholism, drug addiction—all conspire to make a brief professional life even shorter. At the end—in middle age—every player knows something of the pathos found in the story of Early Wynn, a pitcher with 299 lifetime wins— old, overweight, and worn-out—getting battered game after game on his humiliating quest for the magic 300th victory. There's no ballplayer in the game to whom the death of Willy Loman would need to be explained.

The monologues in this collection reflect the morally complex, spiritually challenging, and physically astonishing world of baseball—which is, of course, itself a reflection of the society that developed it. It's a sport that embraces past and present with equal ease, and that opens out forever from the focus of home plate toward the future's infinite outfield. I hope you enjoy what these writers have drawn from its anger and joy and foolishness. Whatever it is, it is as American as Germany Schaefer, who once, in a major league game, lit out from second base with a whoop, ran as fast as God would let him, and made a perfect slide into first.

Old-Timers Game

LEE BLESSING

HARLY *(Rising):* I am a catcher. A catcher is more than his hitting. I'm the leader on that field. I got a million duties. I call
every pitch. I have to think about the hitter, the pitcher, the
ump, the manager, the score, the count, what inning we're
in—all of it. And I get injured a lot. Foul tips. I split my
fingers. I get it in the head, in the face, in the feet. I gotta
squat. I carry a ton of equipment. It's hot. And I never com-
plain. *(Sits again)* And somehow—I don't know how—I still
have enough energy to pull a few jokes on you candyass bas-
tards. Do I get any thanks? No. I'm unappreciated. It was the
same on the big club. I drove the manager nuts, that's for
sure. You know, you're kind of like him. Nervous, tight.
Every day I ask myself, how can I loosen up old Sut? Make
him play loose and carefree—not all squinched up out there
in right.

Shoeless Joe

ALAN THURSTON

JOE: This TV producer called me, askin' if I'd like to come outta "see-clusion." Didn't know I was "see-cluded." I wish I could-da done that TV show but the old ticker gave out. I'dda been gracious, smiled, and thanked everyone who made it possible 'n' all that. But the thing that made me mad was this was jus' the Cleveland Indians Hall of Fame they was puttin' me in. Hell, everyone knows I was good enough for the regular Hall, that one up in Cooperstown. Player like me comes along once in fifty years 'n' nobody that ever lived ever hit the ball harder or threw it further. I was the greatest natural hitter ever. I didn't get none of them squirrelly hits like Cobb 'n' some of 'em others. I never went for that "Hit 'em where they ain't" kindda nonsense. But the thing I'm most proudest of ain't my feats on the ballfield. I'm real happy 'bout how I lived my life after the big scandal. We weren't rich, Katie 'n' me, but we did jus' fine, thank you very much. And my liquor store, it weren't no dump like Cobb said. And I raised my brother's boy! He turned out real fine. I think I'm proud-er of that than anything else . . . I heard that there was some that wanted to scratch my records outta the record books 'n' pretend like I never existed. Even if they had, there wouldda been somebody who wouldda remembered. Maybe even wondered if Old Joe mightta gotten hisself a raw deal. Yeah, I wish I couldda done that TV show. And if they'dda wanted me to say it ain't so, I'dda said it. Said it any way, in any lan-guage, they'dda wanted to hear.

Rain and Darkness

HEATHER MCDONALD

EMMALINE: It was a good night to be at the park. I always liked the way the light goes down the last days of the season. They'd gone eleven innings with no hits. Time was suspended. There was an air of anticipation. It was my mother's last game. It was a hot night. Muggy. Trout La Rue from New Orleans was hitting next. The ballpark in Cleveland was down by the lake and sometimes these feathery white insects would come in off the lake. We called them Canadian Snowballs. It was like the air was full of snowflakes blanketing the field.

Then Williams was up again. He turned and winked at Daddy. The insects were floating softly all around our heads. Like the silence of an early snow. And then everyone in the stands just started singing together, "The weather outside is frightful, and I am so delightful, keeping me safe and warm, let it snow, let it snow, let it snow." Then we heard the crack of the bat and Williams took off toward first, but no one ever saw the ball. No one. Williams rounded the bases and when he landed on home, my dad and Ted Williams fell on the plate hugging each other and laughing.

The next day there was a photograph in the newspaper where it looked like the air was filled with hundreds of floating baseballs. But when you looked more closely, you could make out two actual baseballs captured in the midst of what looked like a snowstorm. One baseball was right at Williams's bat, and the other was caught in flight arcing in a blur across the sky. Two balls in two places in exactly the same moment. The camera had caught time.

Elegy for the House That Ruth Built, and the Game That He Knew

ARTHUR KOPIT

In the dark, we hear the opening music to Field of Dreams. *It's a soft, haunting sound. Lights slowly rise on Jerry DiSibio, early thirties, burly. He wears a NY Yankees satin jacket, which he clearly loves. He stares out, as if listening to the music. Then, after a while, he looks out at the audience and says . . .*

JERRY D: The way it happened—I mean, *really* happened—was not even close to what you saw in the papers, or heard on CNN, or Howard Stern, or whatever you employ as your main source of information these days, the Internet maybe— it doesn't matter. The way it ended was just fuckin' weird. *(Pause)*
 And none of us were prepared. *(Pause)*
 Oh, we were prepared for the strike to end. I don't mean that. We may be lousy players but we aren't dumb. We knew what we were getting into. We knew what we were. . . . *We were trespassers on hallowed ground.*
 Or anyway, *once* hallowed ground. *(Pause)*
 Field of Dreams. You ever see that? Well, you should if you haven't. Kevin Costner. It's a fantasy. Well. . . . sort of. But then, what's baseball if it's not a fantasy, right? I got twenty-five hundred bucks a week for living out my fantasy. That, plus this jacket. Not bad for a month's work, huh? *(He models it proudly)* They gave this to us as we were leavin'. Speaking for myself, 'cause I don't know about the other guys, but I hadn't really expected it. I mean, for me, just to

4

be out there, in right field, in Yankee Stadium, practicing for the opener. For that one amazing day. . . .

I'll tell you something, don't quote me now, 'cause like I'll lose whatever meager reputation I have left, but I have gained, through this experience. . . . *(With difficulty)* I have gained respect for George Steinbrenner. Don't laugh! I mean it! 'Cause, first of all, I saw fear in his eyes. *Real* fear. On that day. The day I just spoke of. When I ran in from right field to report on what I'd seen out there—seen and felt—I and my fellow outfielders. . . . *(Pause)*

And later, when we'd *all* come in, because we just couldn't play anymore, the infielders, everyone, you couldn't pay us enough to walk back out. And Mr. Steinbrenner, bless his heart, he tried, he said, okay, how much more do you guys want? As if all we wanted was more money. And we said, no way, Jose. *We are history.*

And he knew then that what I'd just reported was the truth. And he looked out into right field. The wind had come in by then. And he asked for a jacket, a robe, a coat, something to put over him. 'Cause it was suddenly so cold. From sixty degrees down to twenty in like minutes. *But only inside the stadium! (Pause)*

So somebody from the dugout threw up a jacket and some towels and Mr. Steinbrenner wrapped himself up. I could see him shivering. Not just from the cold. But from the fear. And from . . . speaking now for myself . . . 'cause I was shivering too . . . I think it was maybe mostly from the awe. *(Pause)*

And I saw him look out into right field. I'd been the first to sense it. The movement, if you can call it that, sort of went from right field to left. And he looked out into right field. . . .

And though I could see the Babe, with his bandy legs, and round jowly face, I wasn't sure if *he* could. But he could. Because I could see the blood had drained from his face. *(Pause)*

All the players had come out by then. To the steps of the dugout. It was like . . . so silent in the stadium. No wind anywhere. Never heard such a silence. And then, one by one, the players started saying, "I can see 'm! I can see 'm!" 'Cause at first I guess only a few of us could. *(Pause)*

And then I saw DiMaggio, out in center, loping after fly balls none of us could see. Like some great gazelle. Catching one and then another. And Mr. Steinbrenner saw the Jolter too, 'cause he said, "What the fuck's *he* doin' out there? He's not even dead!" I said, "They don't have to be dead to be out there, Mr. Steinbrenner. With all due respect, sir, I think they just have to be *worthy*." *(Pause)*

And then we saw this . . . *haze. (Pause)*

It had settled over the infield. *(Pause)*

And then . . . suddenly it cleared. *(Pause)*

And there was the Scooter. Rizzuto! At short. But young. And at first . . . it was Gehrig. The dimples. I could see the fuckin' dimples in his cheeks! And he looked over at me. And tipped his cap. And smiled. I turned to Mr. Steinbrenner. He could see it, too. And there was a tear in his eye. Maybe it was only from dirt. But I think it was emotion. *(Pause)*

And then, suddenly, the ball was whizzin' around that infield—not the ball we'd all be playing with, but a pale, almost translucent kind of globe. That somehow gave off the most astounding light. Like moonlight. I had never seen anything move so fast in my life. None of us had. . . . *(Pause)*

And then, suddenly, Mr. Steinbrenner seems angry. He points out at the Babe, and DiMag, and the Scooter, "These guys didn't even play together!" he says. "So what the fuck are they doing here now?" He's *offended!* I can't fucking believe it! And then, all at once, I can see that Mr. Steinbrenner is thinkin'. His brows knot up. And a moment later, he says, "Shit. Maybe I can sign 'em. HEY GUYS! COME HERE A SEC!" *(He smiles)* But they pay him no heed. He might as well be shouting at the wind. *(Pause)*

And then . . . as if all this wasn't weird enough already, one of the players on the bench—a replacement guy, like me, but older, in even worse shape, he has this Polaroid camera,

6

he's been askin' guys to take pictures of him when he bats, well he comes out. He's just taken this snapshot of Gehrig smilin'. But the photo—it shows nothing but grass. And he took one of the outfield. Of the Babe, and DiMag. Same thing. Nothing on the photo but grass. And empty stands. Mr. Steinbrenner, who, say what you will, is no dummy, says, "Fuck this. If they don't show up on Polaroids, they probably don't show up on TV either." And that ends his plans for signing them. *(Pause)*

And then—and I know you won't believe this—by the way, I've gotta tell you, you've done really well so far—but, on my word, may God strike me dead, the sky suddenly darkens, it's two in the afternoon, why is the sky so dark? And we look up and see like this like cloud only it's humming. And then we see what it is. It's fuckin' locusts. It's a plague of fuckin' LOCUSTS! And they're all coming down on us like dive bombers. Only . . . it's not us they're after. It's Mr. Steinbrenner. Within seconds, you can hardly see 'm. His voice, muffled from being underneath all these bugs, and muffled by having, I guess—or at least it sounds like that—locusts in his mouth, well, he's barely audible. But it's audible enough. "I'll settle the strike!" he shouts. "I'll settle the strike!" *(Pause. He listens to the music. More calmly)* So anyway, that was the last day we played. Mr. Steinbrenner called us into his office that night. He said he'd spoken to the other owners and that those who had the older ballparks had reported pretty much the same thing happening. Not with the Babe of course. The Babe was ours. But with people like, well, or so he said, Ty Cobb, Tris Speaker, Lefty Gomez, Ted Williams. *(Pause)*

One of the owners, can't remember who, reported that a man in a long black coat had walked across the field to the box where he was sitting and said he was Abner Doubleday . . . and then spit out this big black chunk of chewin' tobacco splat in the owner's face. *(Long pause)*

Anyway, that's how it came about—this sudden decision to settle. I figured they'd want us the hell out o' there as quick as possible. We all thought that. No more reminders, thank you very much.

But no. Mr. Steinbrenner said, "Hold up." And he turned to this old guy, he was in charge of equipment, been with the Yankees for years. And he said, "Tommy. Give the boys some jackets."

So I think that Mr. Steinbrenner, underneath it all, is okay. 'Cause he didn't really have to do that, you know. Give us the jackets, I mean. . . . *(Pause. Showing off the jacket)*

It's the real McCoy. Not like you get in Herman's. The stitching's really fabulous. Real satin, too.

He stares out, smiling. The dreamy music of Field of Dreams *continues under for a moment. Then it fades.*

Ted Williams

HOWARD KORDER

A man in his thirties addresses the audience.

MAN: So I went to see my sister, I've been feeling bad about it, not seeing her, it's maybe five or six—it's a while and Ruth was looking good, better, really a lot better, there was none of the, that kind of chemical haze is the way it strikes me, like a smudge in front of her face, like you want to take a rag and wipe the, the . . . anyway, we're talking, a *conversation*, just normal, and suddenly she goes, "There are parts of me I've lost I won't ever see again." And I thought, bingadee-boom, here we go, call the nurse. 'Cause when she says things like that, you don't know, she could be talking about her left foot, a kidney, you can't be sure. There's a history there. So I asked her what she meant. I mean at one time she thought that Alan Greenspan and Patrick Swayze were talking through her Osterizer. And my father getting a phone call from Cementville, Indiana, "We have a young woman here with a hospital ID," and my father, well my father—I'm not talking about my father. Not now. Not yet. My *sister* looks me in the eye, she says, "I think I was being perfectly clear." *Hmmm.* Well, I don't know, maybe it's me. Maybe I'm the one who doesn't get it. Maybe you have to be on controlled levels of Thorazine to see things that clearly. . . .

Anyway, I was late for an appointment. I get to the restaurant, the guy's ready for meltdown, I switch into damage control, I'm sandbagging the levee while he's snapping breadsticks thinking about putting all his toys into his sack and taking his financing back up the chimney. I mean not only do I hit the ground limping here but I don't even get to

9

eat my lunch. Can you think on an empty stomach? That's good. Good for *you*. I don't eat, my mind starts to wander. I start getting pictures of me walking down the street squirting kindergarten classes with a flamethrower. *(Pause)*

I would not do that. Christ. You can't say these things today. You can't say anything except "please" and "may I." I was mugged once, guy stepped out from between two parked cars, gets me in a choke hold, sticks a pistol in my ear, and says, "Give me your money and I won't kill your fucking saggy ass," and I said, "Thank you." Walking down the street, minding my business, someone says he won't kill me *if,* my response: "thank you." So I'm not the person to worry about. Let's establish that. I'm not. . . . *(Pause)*

Anyway, that's not what I wanted to say. What I wanted to say was, was . . . lunch, I didn't eat, pissy mood, one and a half million dollars billable revenue out the door. So I stiff the valet because . . . *because I felt like it* and don't tell me you wouldn't either. Yes, I know it's how he makes his living. Yes, I know about the shadow economy of underpaid immigrants without which our great white nation would collapse like a Malibu beach house. But my aorta is pumping guilt at nine million gallons per minute so please please please cut me some fucking *slack* for one nanosecond. If you would be so kind. Anyway I pull out of the parking lot and get shaved by a DHL van traveling Mach-seven, suddenly I'm gifted with fifteen hundred dollars of front-end damage to my Camry. So that should make you happy. Oh, I hear you. I know what you're saying. "It doesn't matter, it's a company car." Ye-es. *But I'm the company.* The company is me. I'm a small-businessman. Here I am, way down here, living in the floor-boards, fighting enormous spiders with a sewing needle and no retirement plan. So don't concern yourself with *me.* *(Pause)*

But that's not what I want to talk about. I finally get to the lawyers, the Camry is shaking like a stagecoach, some minimum wage messenger with a Turtle-Waxed head and a hoop through his nose says, "You need an alignment." *Yes,* I need an alignment, you future ward of the state, I need an alignment and a sewer cleanout and a mortgage refi and quick strange anonymous sex. What I *have* is a meeting with my ex-wife, her lawyers, my lawyers, maybe lawyers of total strangers for all I know, random drive-by lawyers, and actually everything is very civilized, we're smiling, we're making little jokes, I'm looking at her, my ex, I'm thinking, I'm thinking . . . it wasn't that bad. I mean the last three years were a screaming mutant nightmare polka, but the first six, those six years . . . well, we were different people, right. I don't know who we were. But it's not who we are now. And the people we are now . . . who knows who *they* are. Who knows. *(Pause)* Anyway. . . . *(Pause)*

Anyway, that's not what I want to talk about. I want to talk about, uh. . . . *(Pause)* Well, I couldn't put it off any longer, could I. It had been an absolutely *lovely* day up 'til now. But we have responsibilities. We have the right to bear arms, we have the right to a speedy trial, and we have responsibilities. So I'd blown off dinner with him five, six . . . a lot. Does that make me a monster? No. No, it does not me a monster make. It makes me someone who parks the Camry three blocks away because I just don't want to have to explain my *life* in some Freudian inquisition scenario. Aren't you tired of *explanations?* Aren't you fed up with everyone having *reasons* for everything? I mean that's my father. That's him wrapped up right there in an infallible nutshell. If you must know. He answers the door in his bathrobe and slippers, his fifty-year-old immaculate VA hospital bathrobe from when the Nazis gave him ulcers. I say, I thought we're going out to eat. He goes, I thought so too, but after two hours I couldn't wait. Now you see? I'm supposed to have an "explanation." It's not enough that I stopped for two or three drinks on the way over what with the car and the client and the divorce. No. There has to be some *reason.* What are you watching, I ask. The All-Star Game, he says. In this game the National

League plays the American League. Oh, like I never knew. At no other time of the year, he goes, do these leagues have contact with each other. One might almost say that except for this one sanctioned interlude they are willfully unaware of each other's existence. I say, What about the World Series. That, he goes, that's different. Separate cases entirely. The World Series is a collision. The All-Star Game is a . . . meeting. Across a wide gulf. What's this supposed to be, I say, some fucking metaphor? I'm starving. And don't give me that look. Ted Williams never cursed, he says. How do you know, I say. How do you know what Ted Williams did or did not the fuck do in his off time. How do you know Ted Williams wasn't a goddamn mud-crawling swill-drinking *animal?* You don't. *You do not know shit about Ted Williams. (Pause)*

I go into the kitchen, I find a snack pack of Corn Flakes with a June '89 expiration date and a quart of 1% milk. Look, I tell him. Look, I saw Ruth at Cedars Memorial, she seemed better. He keeps on watching the game. Pop, I go, did you hear me? I went to see Ruth. We talked. She's taking her medication. She's doing better. I made a point of seeing her. I took the time. He turns, fixes me with those eyes, those watery old-man eyes, he says, she's not the one I worry about. *(Pause)*

Yeah. Yeah, so. . . . *(Pause)*

. . . I apologized. About Ted Williams. I mean, what the hell, right. Somebody's gotta be good somewhere, it might as well be him. We watched the rest of the game, me and Pop. Could've been worse. But Christ those Corn Flakes sucked.

The Goddess and the Yankee Clipper

LAVONNE MUELLER

ELMORE: I was a movie fan before I was a baseball fan. And that's a hard thing for most of my buddies to understand. 'Cause all anybody hears me talk about nowadays is baseball. But I grew up in Paw Paw, Illinois, first knowing more about movie stars than ball players, being as how we had two movie houses in our town—Big Show One, Big Show Two. Both theatres were really just one old grain storage shed divided by a metal corrugated wall. The music and voices always leaked through. No matter which side you sat on—Big One or Big Two—you were getting two movies at once. And I guess a double dose like that really took and I became virtually a movie fanatic. My favorite star was Marilyn Monroe, and I saw *Seven Year Itch* and *Niagara* at the same time, and I can still repeat every one of her speeches from both films, slicing those silky words thin like an onion, one line of dialogue lying neat and trim up against an alternate line of dialogue so that every movie Marilyn ever made was for me nothing but a perfect Siamese twin performance. A lot of Paw Paw kids saw movie stars that way.

It was Marilyn Monroe marrying Joe DiMaggio that got me into baseball.

The Paw Paw Outlooks were well known in Northern Illinois. Like the mayor always said, their games kept the hoodlums off the street. Moe, my big brother, was their bat boy the year Marilyn and Joe got hitched. Lotta times Moe wouldn't lay all the bats out in a neat row. He was always working on his tan so he'd dump the clubs on the ground and run off to a sunny spot infield. As a result, some of the bats would get accidentally crossed and all hell would break loose. Moe eventually lost his job 'cause of that. Nobody's more superstitious than a baseball player. Loaf-Pan Pomeroy never took a bath when he was winning. Me—I always drank cherry Cokes and cherry Kool-Aid when I played. I even drank warm cherry Jell-O before it turned into rubber. Anything with "cherry" in it. And after a while, that worked.

Sometimes Dad and me would go watch Moe carry bats at Rud Freems Field next to the old high school, which had just moved across town to a bigger new high school, when the famous Pearl Button Factory came to Paw Paw. Moe always made a point to tell his friend, Scrags, that we were there. Scrags sold hot dogs even when the National Anthem was being played, and he always gave us a double shot of relish with our order, which made the bun soggy and got Dad madder 'n hell. But like I always said: "Dad, soggy is being treated special. Like a movie star getting them a front row booth at a fancy place like the Princess Villa Motel Restaurant in Earlville."

I never thought much of baseball to begin with. It just didn't have the reality of movies. I ask you, can a baseball field really be a diamond? Is a *walk* really as good as a *hit?* And players fake each other out—stealing bases or pitching trick balls. The true heroes with all bullshit aside are the guys who clean up afterwards and have to deal with the genuine facts of the game—smashed peanut bags, gunnysack cushions, dirty coffee cups, cigarette wrappers, skunk cabbage, a possum head, thermos jugs, and home-made caramels that some mother boiled into little soft balls that are now sticky, half-eaten, and glued to the ground.

Joe DiMaggio had him a movie star face and that of course made baseball seem glamorous to me. That and the fact that Marilyn was now his wife and went to a lot of games with him. And when it gets right down to it, I guess baseball players and movie stars do have a lot in common. I let myself be philosophical about that at the time of my conversion 'cause I'm not the kind of guy who just leaves one obsession for another without some serious consideration.

In the beginning, baseball players were clowns. Acting silly like a stage comic. So they have them some ancient relatives in the movie world. Besides which, even today a ballgame is like an overblown Western. When the guy in the white hat faces the guys in the black hat, both of them with their guns drawn, how's that any different from a batter facing a pitcher? In either case, somebody's gonna get wiped out when it's over.

I later learned that timing is just as important to an actor as it is to a hitter. Knowing when to get a laugh—well, it's just like knowing when you have to hurl yourself into a swing. Not too early. Not too late. Such similarity always made me feel closer to Marilyn.

I'm kinda average. Five feet, ten inches, and 155 pounds. My back isn't hardly big enough for all the letters of "Paw Paw Outlooks." But that didn't stop me from going out for baseball the summer I graduated from high school in 1962.

I don't know what I thought baseball would do for me. Did I think somewhere in the stands, a Marilyn double would see me hit a homer and come down afterwards to kiss me and sweep me into love and excitement? All I know is I told myself: Elmore Vaughn, you're gonna be a hitter for no other reason than the most beautiful woman in the world loves a hitter.

Baseball was something I figured I could pick up pretty fast. Milking cows all the years I was growing up made my arms tough. Years of picking up corn nubbins for the hogs gave me a strong back. And I ate good. We always had us two kinds of pie every meal, even breakfast. And for a more mature touch, I chewed brown stems of flowers to color my saliva so when I spit it looked like tobacco juice.

Paw Paw has them the only ballpark that half the time it's flooded, and half the time it's got tornadoes going through it. But we've never lost a game to the Waterman Fisters or the

Hinckley Big Rock Blasters who have much better grounds and are always bragging on their weather. I couldn't even sit in our digout 'cause it was usually flattened by a morning twister. Our bases to this day are little islands surrounded by muddy water. In fact, the Paw Paw Outlooks perfected running from second to the plate without touching third, since most of the time third was under water and nobody, not even the umpire, ever saw it. Most of our basemen perch on a high spot like gulls. The mayor once had gasoline poured on the field figuring to burn it dry. But the water only boiled up more solid.

Traditionally, our spectators stand in back of the field. That's okay with me except when opposing teams help a hit or hide extra balls in the mud so their side can pick one up fast and fire a throw to first.

Of course tall stories grew up around the Paw Paw Outlooks. But that's only natural. Any ball club worth anything generates stories—some true, some not true. Like fishermen talking about the big one that got away. DiMaggio's father is a fisherman, so I guess Joe appreciates a tall tale when he hears it. But I know one story that is true 'cause I was there when it happened. Hiram Swink's pig wandered on the field and happened to be right in the path of a walloped grounder, and Drill-Pipe Enos grabbed the ball *and* the pig, throwing both of them to the first baseman who slapped a tag on the runner. Saw it myself.

First time I came up to bat we were playing Earlville. I decided to dedicate a hit to Marilyn. Some of the guys laughed at that, even though they, themselves, were dedicating bucking line drives and pop flies to everybody from their dog to their favorite barber or popcorn wagon.

A group of Paw Paw Baptists were out by our hand-operated blinding white scoreboard that day singing "For Jesus is standing at the home plate . . . waiting for you to come in." Season ticket holders were yelling for me to get my front foot out so I could put my butt into the game. All that caused me to squeeze the bat too hard. The pressure shot right up my body till even my eyebrows went stiff. Then I crowded the plate, wrecking any kind of reaction time. The pitcher was looking at me like I was a wild wolf that had just come through his bedroom window. It was easy for him to draw me out to hit a wide one. I swung too soon and pulled the ball foul. I had taken to smoking for my nerves and just before I came up to bat, I sneaked a puff and hid a flaming butt in my belt loop. When I finally struck out, I also caught on fire. That's how I got the nickname "Torch." I didn't smoke no more after that mostly 'cause it cut down on my wind, but the name stuck.

It wasn't the "Mooooooos" and the "Bahhhhhhs" from the Sears Roebuck Mother Store Association that hurt so much. It was knowing I had let Marilyn down. This was a bad year for her without me adding to it. She'd left her third husband and was fired from the movie *Something's Gotta Give*. But there was one happy spot . . . she was seeing DiMaggio again.

After that game, I put up a batting-tee on the barn over-hang. That baseball dangled there taunting me, and I'd whack away at it for hours every day. I also took to wearing lead weights in my shoes. And I carried around a rubber ball, squeezing it to make my wrists stronger.

It took me a while to know I had to keep my lower hand next to the knob on my bat and just relax. 'Cause a bat has to be there like part of your arm grown longer. I started lining up my knuckles on both hands when I gripped. I even prac-ticed Campy's old "foot in the bucket" batting stance. But most important I stopped thinking at the plate 'cause you can't afford to think and bat at the same time.

Game after game and I just couldn't hit. But I always prided myself on receiving a standing boo. Fans took ice outta their soft drinks and threw it at me.

I remember DiMaggio saying he never hit a ball that ever looked like a home run. Well, I could say the same thing. And in my case, it was true.

I wouldn't give up. I hung in there, running wind sprints, doing laps, and shagging fly balls in center field. I kept telling myself—you can only be a rookie once. I renewed my subscription to *Baseball Digest* and talked to every experienced ball player I could find. Then one day, Everett Birdie, our manager, brought in a bazooka he had used as a sergeant in Korea. He said if I didn't hit, he was gonna blast me clear out of Illinois. Birdie laid that thing right across my locker.

The next afternoon, we were playing against the Kewanee Corn Huskers. They were known to file their spikes, juice up the ball, put trick patches on their bats, lower the mound, move in the fences, and tighten up the strike zone. A lotta people consider that cheating, but the Kewanee Corn Huskers called it working for the good of the team. Besides, fans are going to forgive their team for cheating more than they are for losing.

It was my turn up to bat. The famous Pudge Pork Chop Otto was pitching and he could pitch like ten different guys. He got the name "Pork Chop" 'cause he butchered his daddy's pigs in the winter, skinned them, cleaned them, and hung them on his mama's clothesline to dry. When the Otto family wanted chops, all they had to do was just pick one off the line.

There were three aboard. I could see outfielder Cletus Dry-Wall Rummelhart sneaking binoculars out of his pocket so he could steal signs.

I repeated the first principal rule to myself: That guy tossing a ball at you doesn't want you to hit it.

First thing Pork Chop did was call in the outfield 'cause he figured they didn't need to be there. My batting record was well known, and Pork Chop knew he was gonna strike me out fast. Besides, he was always grandstanding for the fans. Then he examined all 108 stitches on the ball, rolling it around in his right palm. He knew the ball was hand-sewed by the Paw Paw Senior Goldies, and if he found any imperfection, he could yell his head off to the umpire. It's no secret that the Senior Goldies are rabid Paw Paw fans.

I had rubbed my bat with a dry meat-bone like DiMaggio so all the little wood pores were closed. The scorching wind was hanging sluggish from an early-morning tornado. Pork Chop had torn off the lower half of both his shirt sleeves and the tops were flapping in the wind, the way he wanted them to do, so I'd be distracted. There was probably pine tar on his glove for a good grip.

We had us the worst umpire in Northern Illinois. Every time he came on the field, the Paw Paw American Legion sang "One Blind Mice." Our first baseman, Bud "Shards" Odegaard, was already thrown out for arguing. I yelled to the rest of the guys to keep their mouth shut.

It was a 1–0 lead after the sixth, a Paw Paw trademark of on-the-edge-of-your-seat delirium.

I thought of Marilyn's beautiful eyes and how she used them to act. And I knew the "eyes" are the secret for a hitter, too. I had to see the ball as long as I could. What I couldn't see, I couldn't hit. No matter how good the arm muscles. I tried to keep my head from moving, but it was hard since the Kewanee Moose Mothers were famous for flashing mirrors at us, and I was twitching from scattershot glares. I studied Pork Chop, trying to remember how he got me out the last time. I kept my bat from hanging on my shoulder and watched Pork Chop do a final windmill. Like DiMaggio says, if you're going for distance, you almost gotta bat before the pitch is ever released. I waited. Then . . . it came at me looking as tiny as an aspirin—100 miles an hour. A quick snap of the wrists and a cracking sound of my bat. Then silence. Sometimes, there's a couple of seconds when even the fans are quiet. In the name of drama. Like when Marilyn gets a close-up and tells you a secret. That ball went up and suddenly hung lifeless over Paw Paw like a day star. Kewanee fielders were frantically running under it, and for a minute, it looked like they were gonna make a catch. But the good old Paw Paw wind charged up and helped that ball over the scoreboard into

Gus Laberta's backyard pasture, hitting the rear of his old horse, Cora, standing out in the wind with a bald tail blowing up under her belly. Bouncing off Cora, it then rolled twenty more feet across Gus Laberta's unhemmed undershorts washed and spread out on the grass to dry, finally coming to a stop in front of Melba Laberta, who was rolling biscuits with a fresh ear of corn on her back porch. A lotta hits like that in Earlville wouldn't get you to second.

After that game, my confidence was high, and nobody could hold me back. I got good wood on the ball every time I was up to bat. It was like DiMaggio's fifty-six-game consecutive hitting streak back in 1941. The Torch was finally a great slugger. For Marilyn.

I started autographing baseballs and showing off all the bruises I got sliding into home. I guess I was pretty cocky, hanging the pinkie finger of my lower hand off the bat to get some World Series leverage. But I became a better slugger 'cause I wasn't so desperate. I didn't try to hit every pitch.

But like DiMaggio knew, and I knew, too, a hitting streak doesn't last. Even the greats don't hit four times outta ten. I wasn't working with great odds. But I became pretty philosophical on that score. 'Cause the way I figured it—every hitter gets just so many balls he's gonna miss, and there's no sense in going up against fate.

The one good thing about baseball is that you don't need some fancy critic telling you just how good or bad you are. Like the half-wits saying Marilyn was washed up or just a dumb blond with no talent when I know for a fact that she's a great actress. In baseball, all you do is look at the scorecard. All you gotta do is check the numbers. Nobody can cheat you out of a good record like they can with an actor.

It was August 1st that summer of 1962 when my brother Moe, now a pipe fitter in Harvey, Illinois, told me his old vendor friend had gone on to the Big Leagues. Scrags, who always gave us too much relish, was hawking peanuts and dogs for the Yankees.

Scrags called one Monday to tell us that Joe and Marilyn were coming to Yankee Stadium that Saturday. He'd heard it from one of the ground crew whose sister was married to Joe's barber. If we wanted to see them, he could get us in.

Did I want to see them!

Moe had to work, but Paw Paw wasn't playing that day, so I got me a midnight Greyhound express from Chicago to New York City. Mom packed fried mush, hominy pudding, her famous tapioca, fist-sized biscuits and pumpkin butter in an old polished Karo syrup can. But I was so excited I couldn't eat.

Scrags met me at the bus station and took me to his one-room apartment in the Bronx. We both suited up. If I wanted to get close to Marilyn and Joe, I had to wear a silly hat and vest and sell hot dogs with him, though he warned me I'd be working in a place as big as that Roman Coliseum we read about in Miss Stoppelmoor's history class, and I'd probably end up with gladiator-type blisters all over my feet. But Marilyn and Joe had third base box seats in his territory, and if I was lucky, they'd buy something off of me.

Scrags sat me on an old sofa whose entrails were dragging on the floor and told me not to embarrass him if I did get lucky. "It's pronounced *Di-mah-zhee-o* not *DeeeeMadge-ee-o,*" he said. Then we each drank a glass of water from an old Cracker Jack box because it was hot and we had to guard ourselves against dehydration 'cause even the butter he had left out on the table had turned to oil.

The only way Scrags had to get rid of flies was tearing an old rag into strips and nailing it to a broomstick. He kept flapping that broomstick all over the room. He said the thing he missed most about his home place in Paw Paw was tossing curveballs to the barn kittens.

I offered him some of Mom's famous tapioca, but he said he couldn't eat anything that looked like fish eyes. I handed over the other stuff Mom had cooked, but he refused. Most of the time, he just ate Corn Flakes. His profession had turned him off of good food forever. 'Cause of the trash he had to deal with. Not that he was complaining. This was the big time. And he learned a lot. He could measure the success of any game by the smashed paper cups and candy wrappers left in the stands. Like two hundred Milky Ways to a hit. Five hundred Cokes to a triple. Two thousand peanut shells for a homer.

We got to Yankee Stadium early. There were hundreds of buses lined up outside. I just stood in awe, dwarfed by the most important piece of property in the whole world—161st Street and River Avenue.

The bleachers were jammed. It was like all of New York was here, the state itself like a neighborhood. I looked down, past a group of women with T-shirts that said "Mantle is my summer," to the diamond where DiMaggio's famous hitting streak had first started. The bases looked so white and clean.

It was the Yankees against Chicago. Mantle was going to do some hitting, and Yogi was scheduled for a little outfield-ing. I didn't know it at the time, but Yogi only had another year to go.

Scrags showed me how to walk carrying the vending tray on my hip, keeping my right arm clear for handing out the franks and taking the money. Then he showed me DiMaggio's box seat. I walked over and touched it for luck.

Fans hollered for service. They wanted the poisonous greasy red-hots before they even sat down. I was working both hands. Scrags was even putting his head and shoulders into the job, pushing along paper cups of Coke with his chin. He could pitch a bag of peanuts over fifty rows. Scrags warned me that a seller had to have "muscle memory" like a ball player and build himself up to the point where the mus-cles know how to act automatically. "Good vendors oughta have their own baseball cards," he said, "'cause this is really their stadium—baseball players come and go."

The place got so packed, fans had to hold hot dogs over their heads to sidestep into a seat. Spillover crowds were standing in the ramps. A fistfight broke out between a shirt saying, "I ate 1,000 hot dogs at Yankee Stadium" and a red baseball hat with the word "Yogi." Thanks to the rough-housing, I got a precious piece of broken bleacher to take home.

Then I saw them. DiMaggio and Marilyn. They walked down the steps to their box like a king and queen. Nobody dared to push or shove anywhere near them. Even with the heat, DiMaggio wore an elegant pin-striped suit—like he was reminding us that his off-field uniform was only slightly different from his on-field uniform. He was still the Jolter. Marilyn was wearing a blue polka-dot dress, low in front and very fizzy.

I don't know how I kept my mind on giving back the right change. I do know, I never saw much of the game. At one time, half the bleachers stood up and yelled: "Strike the bum out." But I was too busy to see who they were screaming at.

In the sixth, Marilyn lifted her hand. One finger was beckoning me. Scrags gave me a push towards their box seat. At first I was paralyzed. Nothing worked. Not even my eyelids. Scrags pushed me again. My cheeks were hot. A little kid was licking Cracker Jacks and sticking them one by one on my pants leg like cowboy studs. My hair was damp and smelled like oil cloth. And there I was—standing in front of the Goddess and the Yankee Clipper.

"Can I just have a hot dog bun?" Her voice was lavender and sticky like cotton candy.

"Ah . . . ah . . . yah, I guess so," I stuttered.

"I'm on a diet."

"Miss Monroe will have a bun. Give me a Coke."

"Yes, Mr. Deeee-Madge-ee-o," I said. The Jolter winced.

What was I gonna do with the frank? Scrags hadn't briefed me on this emergency. Does she still want mustard on the bun? The works, including pickles? How much do I charge for a bun?

I extracted the unwanted wiener from its casing, all gooey from catsup, and slapped it on top of the peanut bags like a wounded beach eel. I was trying to hide it under some napkins when suddenly Mantle cracked a homer—the ball's great curving arch moving out of the park. Section 130 started a stopwatch chant to see if Mantle could break the record for the slowest home-run trot. I stood in awe as he went around the bases, swinging his bat like Charlie Chaplin's cane. All the fans in the left field bowed down to him, screaming, "Mantle. Mantle."

Marilyn and Joe stood up in all the excitement, and she leaned against him, smiling. Then I heard her whisper, "Oh, Joe. Joe." His famous slugger arm was around her waist. In all the excitement, I was able to move in close, so close I was plastered up against them holding out a bun and Coke like some reverent altar offering. And then she said—in the breathy other-worldly way that was now very real—"If you die before me, I'll hit a high one over your grave."

If DiMaggio said anything after that, I didn't hear him. He just took the bun and Coke from me and tossed a five dollar bill on the tray. He wouldn't accept change.

After the game was over, I sat in the stands watching the exact spot where they both had been. The electronic scoreboard read: "Goodbye Joe." I couldn't get her words out of my head . . . "I'll hit a high one over your grave." And I thought then and there, it's wonderful how baseball is about so many things besides baseball.

At the end of the season, I quit the Outlooks. Cold turkey. What was the use of going through my up-and-coming slump like DiMaggio had to go through his. Besides, a baseball career is a short career. Mine just happened to be shorter than most.

Of course, Marilyn never did get a chance to hit a "high one" over DiMaggio's grave. 'Cause she died before him. Way before him. In that August of 1962. And with her gone, I lost my incentive to hit.

After I quit playing ball, the Yankees took a terrible dive. Scrags got bumped back to the minors. DiMaggio began to do Brylcreem commercials. I teamed up with Dad to farm.

I still have the piece of broken bleacher from Yankee Stadium. Here, you can touch it. Next week, I'm giving it to the DeKalb County Court House for their padlocked glass case. Once it's in there, you won't be able to feel history with your own hands.

I've been dating a lotta different girls over the last year and a half, taking them to see all the games the Outlooks play. Seems like I just can't stick to one of them. I guess I'm destined to live out my life alone. 'Cause I knew that day when I left Yankee Stadium just as sure as I know now, I'll never find me a woman in Paw Paw or the whole world who can love me like that over my grave when I die.

Pride Goeth

KENNETH ROBBINS

Dolph DeSmet is a young man in his early twenties. He is dressed in black pants, a white long-sleeved dress shirt, and a black four-in-hand tie. His bicycle is propped against a fence. From his backpack he takes a copy of the Book of Mormon and a baseball and glove. He bounces the ball against the fence and catches it. He addresses us.

DOLPH DE SMET: There's this thing out in the Black Hills. A carving. You've seen it? Teddy Roosevelt trying to hide; he knows he doesn't belong up there. Lincoln in his humility, looking wise. Jefferson with this look of curiosity. And Washington. Washington, the image of pride. That Sunday afternoon when the Cougars and the Treetoppers squared off for the baseball championship of the Cs, a game played in the unpaved parking lot of Mount Rushmore, I didn't play. I think Washington understood why. And won't leave me alone about it. *(He holds up his Book of Mormon)*

It rained on Saturday. Can you believe that? Never fails, always rains on Saturdays, and that means. . . . Well, baseball and Sundays don't mix. Mormons don't play ball on Sundays. I'm a Mormon. *(Takes a baseball jersey from his backpack and puts it on, leaving it unbuttoned. The "Cou" on one side, "gars" on the other. He points to the word as he says)* Cou-gars. The Iron Mountain Cooooou-gaaaars. Great bunch of boys, those guys. Best nine-man lineup in the Corps. Almost. Oh, yeah, we played ball in the Crops. It wasn't all fighting fires and planting trees. Those nine guys. . . . They were the best! Well, nearly the best! Cage on first, didn't miss much. Roy Martin on second, good range, weak arm, and an asshole city slicker, but we didn't care about that. Good eye, walked a lot. The Boot at short, until Cracker came along. Cracker, heart of the team, firebrand from Georgia with enough cockiness to fill every last one of us with sass. But could he hit? God, could he hit. He turned Boot into Water Boy. Glove at third and Fleet in left. Fleet could have played for any double-A team in the country, only he wasn't too bright. Like he'd steal second with two out in the bottom of the ninth and the Cougars six runs behind, or make a perfect throw to first while a run scored from third. Woody in center, backup pitcher, just in case? JoJo in right. We prayed nobody'd hit anything to right. Marv behind the plate, and me on the mound. Ol' Marv. Face black and blue from all those foul tips until we got him a mask mid-season. Nobody stole on Marv. Put it in Cracker's back pocket and never come up from the knees. God, great bunch. Yeah, the almost best team in the CCCs. *(He pulls from his pack a well-worn ball cap with the letters* IM *stenciled on it. He refers to the letters)* Yeah. Pride all over the place. IM. Short for I am. I am what? All season long, I wore this cap and forgot all about it standing for Iron Mountain. Instead, it stood for me. I am. *(Puts the cap on)*

Pride. A canker in a man's soul. Right, Mr. Washington? Old stone face never answers. *(He becomes a pitcher, winds, throws the ball against the fence. Catches the rebound)* We— the Cougars—the I-am team of 1936—got through the summer with just one loss, that to the Treetoppers of Pine Creek. We could beat them. No doubt about it. With me pitching? Sure thing. First time we played? Cracker was still in Georgia. Second time—well, we had us a secret weapon in our shortstop's bat. We came to the last game of the season needing the win to be champeens of the Hills. Oh, boy, that sounded good: Civilian Conservation Corps Black Hills Regional Baseball Champions! Only to do that, we had to whip the Treetoppers—in their backyard. *(He bangs the ball into his glove)*

27

And the Saturday of the game? Rained all night Friday, well into Saturday morning. When the CO called the team together and said, game's tomorrow. . . . Well, I'm Mormon. Mormons don't play ball on Sundays. I told him so, too, and he wanted to know about Cougar pride, pride of the Corps, and all that. I had nothing to say to him but "Pride goeth before the fall." *(He puts his glove in his backpack and holds his Book of Mormon)*

They came at me. I was letting the guys down. I knew that. Didn't have to tell me that. Without me on the mound, what chance did we have? That's not pride, is it? I mean, I understood. Even with me on the mound, what chance was there? Pine Creek was a different bunch, made up of old-timers, ex service men who had nothing better to do than play ball for a CO who didn't care what he did to win that championship. I knew all that. Still, Iron Mountain's one moment of possible glory, and what was I doing about it? Shooting it in the foot. *(He thumbs through the book before slamming it closed)*

Oh, it was Cracker who argued the most. It wasn't that I was letting our CO down, or Cougar pride, or anything like that. No. Cracker cheated. He laid it on the line: I was letting him down, him personally. Just him, nobody else. And why? 'Cause I'm Mormon? Said that was what he couldn't under-stand, so I asked him, wasn't he a Baptist? And he said, sure, so long as it suited him. I asked him what he believed in, and he told me: baseball, his family, his girlfriend, maggots, and baseball. *(Takes off his cap and holds it)*

I don't know. If you believe something, you believe it. You don't believe it when it's convenient or when you feel like it. I believe that the Sabbath is holy. I believed it then, believe it now. If it's holy, it should be treated that way. You know, holy. You can't change what you believe just because it hap-pens to rain on Saturday or because your pals need you to play a game of ball. If you believe something, that's all there is to it. I don't ask anybody to believe the same as me, though

I'd like it if they did. Believe what you want and leave me alone, okay? *(Puts cap away)*

So I sat in Iron Mountain that Sunday afternoon and let the guys play their ball without me. I remember giving Cracker my blessing: may you go six for six and return the conquering hero. And he said, fat chance. *(Takes off the jersey and puts it away)*

Actually, I couldn't stay behind. I can conquer pride but not curiosity! That Sunday was a beaut, and there wasn't anything in the church that said a body couldn't go to a game. So I tagged along. They played in the half-finished parking lot at Mount Rushmore. With George Washington looking on! The two days of rain had left the field one big mud puddle. Nobody seemed to mind. It didn't matter anyway. Halfway through the first inning after the Treetoppers had scored their first five runs, Cracker took off his shoes and played barefoot, the way they played ball back home, he said. Mud squished between his toes. He called it "cutting his feet." After that, it was all fun and games. It didn't matter that the Cougars got beat eighteen to two, or that the game got called in the middle of the sixth because of a sudden thunderstorm. What mattered was, everybody had a good time and went home happy. 'Cept me. I was the only Cougar who didn't get his feet cut that Sunday afternoon. *(He puts his backpack on)*

George Washington sat up there on the side of that mountain with a tilted head and a little smirk on his face. It looked to me like he knew a whole lot more than he was telling us. Like he understood. "Pride goeth. . . ." Yeah, I think he knew something even now I'm not sure I understand. Pride goeth . . . and then we fall. *(He shakes his head)*

There were more Mormons than me around that ball game on Sunday afternoon. They played for the Treetoppers. George Washington knew that. That smirk on his face? I think it was meant for me. *(Long pause)*

I ain't played ball since that day. Pride goeth. . . .

Dodger Blue

MERRY ELLEFSON AND TOM LINKLATER

*Duke, a Yup'ik, and Bonnie, an Athabascan, are finishing up
dishes in a creek near the cabin.*

DUKE: My father and the elders used to sit and listen to the
World Series games on Armed Forces radio. They liked to
hear the voices that came out of that little box. Grandpa'd
turn the knob and there'd be a different voice—like magic.

Dad rooted for the Dodgers because they were the under-
dogs. He loved Roy Campanella and Pee Wee Reese, but his
favorite player was Duke Snider. And then in 1955, the
Dodgers finally won their first World Series and beat the
Yankees. Duke Snider hit four home runs and he and Johnny
Podres were the big heroes. So when I was born a few weeks
later, I got my native name, Cukuyaq, but Dad also called me
Duke. But two years after they won, the owner moved them
to LA so he could make more money. Typical gossack. Then
they came in and demolished Ebbets Field, their home. But
Dad, he still loves Dodger blue. He doesn't care who owns
what, they're just his favorite team.

i dreamed i was a baseball card

RICHARD STOCKTON RAND

In the darkness we hear the following play-by-play: "What a spot. Mickey Mantle, who is one for three today, is now batting left-handed against the rightie, Camillo Pasqual. Pasqual gets the sign. The runners lead off first and second. The pitch to Mickey. High and tight. Ball two. Mickey Mantle needs one more hit to tie Joe DiMaggio for third place behind Gehrig and Ruth for the most hits of any Yankee. All right. The Yankees with good speed on the basepaths. Mantle digging in. Here's the pitch by Pasqual—HOLY COW! A home run for Mantle! HOLY COW, an upper-deck shot for Mickey Mantle! And the crowd is going wild as Mickey has just hit one nine miles in the upper deck! The crowd is on their feet cheering for their hero, Mickey Mantle, as the Yankees win it on a three-run homer, four to one." *Lights up on a boy in a New York Yankees baseball uniform.*

BOY: I dreamed I was a baseball card. *(Thousands of baseball cards fall from the sky. Blackout)* I dreamed . . . *(Lights up on the boy in the batter's box. He swings in slow motion at the oncoming pitch. Blackout)* I was a baseball card. *(Lights up on the boy poised with a mitt. In slow motion, he dives backhand for ball hit down the line. Blackout)* A baseball card. *(Lights up)* You start completely still. See him in your hand. Looking up at you. Flip. *(He begins flipping baseball cards)* Heads. See him. Flip. Heads. Color faces. Flip. Heads. Heroes of the game. Heads. It's in the fingers. Heads. Always the same. Heads. Never tails. Heads. Only faces. Heads. Forever. Heads. Mounds of baseball cards looking up at you. Take 'em home. Put 'em in a shoebox. Hide 'em under the bed—where I listened to them Yankees on my transistor radio, 'cause my father didn't trust baseball. I'd listen under the bed to night games at the Stadium. It was like being down in the Yankee dugout with the sound of a million people echoing in your ears. My sister could hear the crowd cheering clear out of my earplug. "The Mick just hit one out," I'd say. That's Mick— The Mick. *(He steps into the spotlight)*

Mickey Mantle. Born on October 29, 1931, in Spavinaw, Oklahoma, the son of a miner. It would be many years before Mickey would engrave his most spectacular feats into the record books. As a boy, he had been the victim of a deadly bone disease. However, through drugs, medical treatments, and a high tolerance for pain, he would overcome this and become one of the most stupendous players ever to don a uniform. Among his many records, he will be especially remembered as the youngest player ever to win the Most Valuable Player Award. And though tragedy befell him on a rainy summer's afternoon when he stepped through the sod and caught his ankle while chasing a fly ball, Mickey overcame this injury as he did every trial he faced, and went on to become a legend of the playing field. Though he hobbled to the plate in excruciating agony for the rest of this life, The Mick never failed to give his all, hitting some of the longest home runs in baseball history. *(He steps forward out of the spotlight)*

When he steps up, you're thinking, "Home run, home run, home run." Everybody's thinking, "Home run, home run, home run." The hush of the crowd, the voice of the Ole Redhead. *"Full count on Mantle."* If you think hard enough . . . *"The pitch—"* you can make it happen. *"And Mantle swings. It's a fly to deep right field. He's going back, back, back. OHhhhOHH! DOCTOR! IT'S OUTTAhere! Mantle wins the game in the bottom of the ninth inning."* It works, too. That was me as Ole Red. . . . The Redhead— Red Barber, and I was honing my play-by-play skills— *"Game seven of the World Series. Bottom of the ninth, Yankees* up *by one and it's a hard grounder to Coleman, over to Rizzuto, back to first, double play!"*—for my future career as a Yankee broadcaster. This is after I got in the Hall of Fame for stealing the most bases 'cause I was fast, you bet, 'specially when I was being chased.

And that's how I found this hiding place. He was looking for me, and I'd *(He slides)* slid under my sister's bed. He was on his way to looking under there. He did look under there. But he didn't see me. Know why? I was invisible. Up 'til then, I'd done a lot of practicing being invisible down the earplug wire into my transistor radio, or inside the pocket of my baseball mitt. That's where you catch 'em . . . in the pocket. *(He enacts the following)* "It's hit. You're after it. Diving in the hole, you got it. The throw . . . it's in the air . . . floating. He's running. You just watch. . . . hope."* I'd dream all night of diving catches and game-winning plays. Then, in the morning I'd jump out of bed and start running. *(He enacts)* "He flies down the stairs, rounds the kitchen, he's into the dining room. It's gonna be close. (He slides) HE'S SAFE! at the couch."* But in winter when I couldn't get out, I needed a secret hiding place. That's how I found *this* place. My Dad was looking for me and I slid under my sister's bed. And there was this rip in the box spring I could squeeze through perfect like a secret passage. *(He climbs into imaginary box spring)* What a place! There were globs of cotton with springs sticking through 'em and these boards I could lie down on perfect. And nobody found me. Never. Not ever. They looked, too. But I was invisible. Inside the box spring I could sleep safe with my transistor radio, and I'd dream I was a baseball card living inside the Hall of Fame—which is like heaven for baseball players. I'd spend all night seeing the stats on the back of my baseball card, remembering each and every base hit 'til I fell asleep. That's how I saved myself.

(He picks up bat) Being invisible paid off in Little League, too. I was number seven. Mickey Mantle. Your number's who you are. How to move. How to swing. How to step up to the

plate. Your stance. It was all in the number. Feel the Mick. Number seven on my back and all through me, pinstripes, through my heart—and hurt. The Mick's always hurt. It's in his knees. Can't get out. I was the Mick. And nobody could touch me. Couldn't pitch to me either. Too little. *(He drops into a crouch at the plate)*

It was bases loaded, two outs, bottom of the ninth. And up at bat . . . me. That big guy's getting ready to pitch. Boy, he's fast. Salvatore something's his name. And his face is like a rhinoceros. Parents are screaming at the fence. My manager's clapping down the third-base coach's box. I'm trying to dig in. The catcher's yelling, "He can't hit it!" through his mask. The ump's wiping off home plate. Salvatore's ready. Nods. Winds. Fast, whizzing past me. "Ball One!" the ump yells. My heart's pounding. My manager's down from third. He whispers, "Take the pitch." That means don't swing. I step back like I'm going to hit, but I'm just faking. He nods. He winds. It's fast, past my head. *(He hits the dirt)* "Ball Two!" the ump yells. The other team screams, "Chicken!" They're right, too. He's ready. Gets the sign. It's coming. . . . OUTside, WAY outside! Three balls! One more. I drop the bat. Walk down the line. Touch first. We win. Just one more ball. But I didn't do nothing. They're all yelling, "Chicken!" It's 3 and 0. He's going to lay it right down the middle. I could hit it, if it's in, I could hit it. He gets the sign. He's winding up. I know I can hit it. *(He swings)* "Strike One!" "Let it go!" my manager screams. Why'd I swing!? They're laughing at me. Why'd I swing? He's ready again. Sign from the catcher. He starts the wind-up. It's . . . outside. Strike!? It was outside! "Full count!" the ump yells. This is it. He's staring in. I'm staring at him. The whole field's like nobody's breathing. Count's full. Three and two. This is it. Then it gets quiet all of a sudden. And I see Mickey Mantle like a giant baseball card in center field. And he's smiling at me. And it's like Salvatore was just some guy . . . like me, 'cept I'm bigger. I see the ball in his hand and his rhinoceros face and he's scared. He starts to wind up. It's like slow motion. See the ball coming at me like the whole world. Like I can't miss. *(He swings)* It's hit! Hard! Flying out to center, rolling to the wall. *(He runs the bases)* I'm digging, 'round first, going for two. They stop. I look around. We won! I won it! They're coming to get me like I'm the hero!

But that's not what happened. I let the next pitch go. It was high and outside. Dropped the bat. Walked to first. The guy on third touched home. We won. They lifted me up but I didn't deserve it. I was chicken. The other team said so. I was, too, and too little to do any good. . . . 'til I remembered my secret weapon. . . .

(He sits and picks up baseball from mitt) My ability to throw a round object through the air and hit a desired target was a genetic trait and quite remarkable. I saw them through the doorway.

The shadows of two figures are seen on the back wall.

His face was close to hers. It was twisting and making loud sounds. His hands shook her and her head bounced back and forth. There was a round object in my hand. I think I mentioned that. I knew what I had to do. Fastball. STEEERIKE! It was quite remarkable—my secret weapon.

The shadows disappear.

(He demonstrates) Pitching's 98 percent of the game. To be a good pitcher you have to have good stuff and good control. And you got to be fast. *(He pitches)* STEEERIIIKE! Fastball is the number one pitch. You can throw it high and hard, low and away, or with some mustard on it. *(He pitches)* STEEERII-IKE! Control is important, too. You got to be able to hit a corner, keep 'em guessing, and know when to knock him down. STEEERIIIKE! Most important, you got to have a bread-and-butter pitch. Curveball. *(He pitches)* STEEERIIIIKE! It was

magic. You feel it in your hand, turning it over. Find the seams, your fingers together. Feel the fingertips. With the fastball that's the last to touch. But not the curve. The curve slides off the side, spinning like a tornado, the bat swinging where it was *(He pitches), STEEERIIIKE!* but it ain't there. *(He steps off the mound, rubs the ball up)* When we were in trouble, I step to the mound. I was the short man. The Stopper. Got the ball in my hand. Turning. I look in to home. See his face. I knew what I had to do. Fastball. *(He pitches) STEEERIIIKE!* Then I knew being little meant something.

I practiced pitching in my room 'til Mom'd say goodnight. Then, I'd sneak into my sister's room, squeeze into the box spring and turn invisible. Only me, my baseball cards, and the voice of Yankee broadcaster Red Barber, from the cabbage patch, coming through the earplug. My sister and I talked to each other through the mattress while they were fighting downstairs. I'd tell her how the game's going like the Ole Redhead: *"It's back, back, back, back. It's, it's, it's—- Ohhhhh-HO, Doctor! Mantle flags it down by the monuments. Another Yankee victory tied up in a crocus sack!"* And they'd leave us alone, 'cause we never made no noise, 'til one night. But before then, being in the bed was like being in Yankee Stadium. I'd follow the game and put the Yankees baseball cards on me like I was the baseball field. *(He puts baseball cards on top of his body)* Mickey was here in center, and in right field, Mickey after he hurt his knees, and on first base, Mickey . . . like before he retired, and at shortstop, Mickey when he was a rookie, and at third, Mickey 'cause he played one game there, and behind the plate . . . Yogi Berra—or, maybe Mickey. And when they was up at bat I'd listen to the Redhead and move all the Mickeys around me. I'd tell my sister, too, like we were there, but we were never there, except that once.

Then, one night . . . he comes in. Just stands there. Could feel him. Thought for sure he'd found me. *(Pause)* But he's watching her. She pretends she's asleep. It was a long time he stayed there . . . breathing. Could hear him . . . breathing. Feel his shadow. Then he walks back downstairs. Kept happening. Then, one night . . . he sits . . . on the edge of her bed, the mattress sagging damn near on top of me. Then, every night he comes up, sits down: same time, Mom's watching Johnny Carson, and he stares at her pretending she's asleep. I hear him breathing. He made a lot of noise when he breathed. Then it starts. He's moving the covers, whispering to her. She's making sounds, like trying not to make sounds. I hear laughing on TV downstairs, springs moving next to me. And the noises. I can't move. The mattress is pressing down on me and they're right there. So I turn invisible . . . like a dot, and slide down the earplug wire into my transistor 'til there's only Yankee Stadium and the crowd screaming in my ear. Then it's over. *(Pause)* The mattress stops. Hear his shoes on the floor and he's down the stairs humming like nothing happened. Mom never says nothing. Just sits watching Johnny Carson. Nobody says nothing. Every night it happens. 'Til once, he's coming up, she says, "What should I do?" "Hide," I tell her. "Where?" she says. "Invisible." "How?" "Little, little, like a dot!" I tell her. But she couldn't do it.

So, it goes on. We listen. Every night. Johnny Carson. And he's up. Out of his chair. Footsteps on the stairs, humming like nothing's going to happen. Then he's there. Big heavy shoes. Staring. Sits. On the edge of her bed. Every night. Then it starts. I don't want to be there, but I couldn't leave her.

Then, she thought of a way. It was getting cold, so she'd stay up all night putting her head out the window. And it worked. She got so sick the doctor quarantined her. Now nobody could touch her. Pretty good thing. We rigged up two cans and a string through the bedroom windows and we planned our escape the whole time. I'd bring her meals up with secret notes under her grapefruit, and she'd roll her pills under the door for me to get rid of. Meals went in and pills came out for months; she stayed sick. She was playing her

37

cards right. Five months without going to school. She learned how to be invisible and now nobody could touch her. And she stayed in there studying and got hundreds on all her exams! Can you believe it? What a genius!

But she started feeling better in the spring and we knew we had to make a getaway plan. We got the idea from this book *The Hobbit* she read for English about two guys that went off to find another world after where they lived stopped being safe. And boy, that sounded right for us. See, this guy Bilbo Baggins was the hero, and he lived in a place under-ground, like a . . . like a dugout. And he was a little guy, like a leprechaun, but baggy. And she reads to me all night about his adventures and we plan our escape.

We decide to write a letter to Mickey and we tell him everything. Then instead of going to school, I take her on the train up to Yankee Stadium. We sit in the bleachers and wait for the Mick to come out and take flies. We got the letter all ready for me to run out onto the field. But he don't come out. It's his knees. My sister and me went back home, but she got real sick from not having been outside all winter. They put her in the hospital. Seventh floor. Mickey's number. Every day they visit. I call on the phone after they leave and she tells me what the doctors say. I told her to take her medi-cine, but she wouldn't. She got so bad they had to put her in tensive care. Said she might die. I thought if he—but he never will. Just sits in his chair all night . . . for months.

Me. I'm down at the park chasing foul balls for the big guys . . . and waiting for a shot. One day I got to run the bases. Next thing I'm playing the fence. *(He grabs mitt)* When they'd hit one over, I'd run it down. *(He enacts)* Tearing through monkey bars, into the sandbox, leaping the benches and into the swings at full speed, my eye on that ball. *(He makes a diving catch)* It was a dangerous job. Then once I hung on to one after running to a monkey bar and I knew I was in. They were all standing over me when I came to. "You little devil, we thought you was dead!" they said. From then on, that was me. LITTLE DEVIL. And I got to play hardball with the big guys. My position . . . the Roof. I could see everything from up there. And nothing could touch me. Being on the roof meant taking homers away from the big guys. It helped if you could see through the incinerator smoke, leap tall buildings in a single bound, and fly onto fire escapes for line drives. And I knew those fire escapes like I was born on them. Chaffey Boy's on the mound. He gets the sign. It's fast. It's hit, blasted back, back to the ball. It's mine, mine! *(He enacts)* Leaping puddles, jumping skylights, running through the smoke, and I'm out, over the edge, three floors up, both of us flying. Hit the next roof and it's there, there, coming down, down, pulling me, taking me, somewhere, to the edge, and over. *(He dives)* I GOT IT! and down, hit the fire escape, the metal sounds like a million people cheering. But I ain't hurt. And I'm up. And nothing can touch me. "ONE OUT!" *(Pause)* Not just anybody could play the roof. Only us leprechauns.

But summer went into fall. The Yankees came in last place for the first time ever. It was the end of the Dynasty. One day, he took me to see her 'cause her brain wasn't remembering things. When I walked in she smiled right off, but no matter what, she couldn't recognize him. Over the next few months she had five operations. The doctors couldn't understand why she kept rejecting her medication. It's 'cause she wasn't taking it! She went into a coma and she'd call out in the night, "Ohhhh-HO Doctor! Going Back, Back, Back, Going, Going—" And me, I prayed to the leprechauns. Then, one day she woke up. And she told me 'bout a dream. She was in great danger. The leprechauns came and took her on the train to heaven—but it's Yankee Stadium! She steps out into a bunch of clouds and this baseball's heading right at her, and it's a Mickey home run. She reaches out to grab it and it's me, my head, inside the baseball, saying, "Don't give up!" She was off and on for months, but she kept coming back.

My mother took me to visit her in the spring. It was a real warm day and they said I could wheel her outside, so I rode her round the bases at the park across the street. She even stole home with the bases loaded. Said it was the happiest day of her life. When we got back the doctor asked her if she wanted to go home and she told him what happened. . . . He must have told my mother 'cause we went home and packed up her stuff quick. Then she flew away . . . with the leprechauns . . .

It was just me then. Alone. Waiting for him. To find out. I hear the garage. Then he comes up, asks how she is. It's quiet. Something's going to happen. I'm waiting. She must be telling him. He starts moving . . . FAST! DOORS SLAMMING! Then. PLATES HITTING THE WALL. I feel 'em shake 'til there's no more plates. Then, he's up the stairs, in her room, pulling drawers out, sees her clothes gone, slams her door OVER 'N OVER. Doors slamming OVER 'N OVER. Then he's down, down to get her. "Don't touch me!" she says. "I know what happened." *(Pause)* That stops him. Then nothing.

Nothing. He just sits in the kitchen all night, eating oatmeal and reading the paper with the news on. *(He sings)* *"W.I.N.S. WINS Radio 78. de,de,de,de,de,de,de,de,de,de,de,de. You give us 22 minutes, we'll give you the world. NEXT UP, YANKEE HIGHLIGHTS!"* CLICK. Something about them Yankees he didn't like. I stare at him through the floor. He stares at me. Right through the floor. Looking into each other's head. But he don't like what's in mine. So he huddles over his oatmeal, grumbling curses under his breath. I hear 'em through the radiator . . . the sounds going 'round in the pipes, sometimes loud, sometimes soft; it felt sort of good always being there in my sleep. But when there was quiet, too much quiet, something's going to happen. I knew it. So I had to listen. *Beep.* Like radar. For when it happened. *Beep Beep.* I can feel him. *Beep.* Track him. *Beep.* Through the floor. *Beep Beep.* Like a bomb. Moving. Then the doors start—*SLAM!*

Over and over—*SLAM!* All night—*SLAM!* But, I'm ready for him *(He picks up bat)*, holding the bat, case he comes in. *SWING!* I practice in the dark. *SWING!* See his face moving. *SWING!* The words coming out of his mouth. *SWING!* And his head flies out the window, over the rooftops and into the galaxy. *(Pause)* Finally, he puts his bowl in the sink, hums this song, just kind of hums it out of his neck, 'cause he's got no head *(He hums "Summertime . . . and the livin' is easy")*, yawns like somebody falling off a roof *(He yawns as his father yawns)*, but without the "KKKHHH!!" then walks up the stairs—one step, listen, 'nother—listen, 'nother—listen, 'nother—listen. Stops. Breathes. *(He breathes as his father breathes)* Another step, listen, step, step, step, 'nother step—CREAK! one more step. Stops at the top. See him through the door. What's he stopped for? What's he thinking? Step. Step. Step. Turns the handle. Door creaks. He shuts his door. And I'm safe.

And I'm out. Out of bed. Sneakers on. Quiet! Open my door—quick! On the stairs, slow. One step. Listen. 'Nother. Listen. 'Nother. Listen. Then—down, down, down, down, down, down, down, down. Stop. Listen. In the kitchen. Close the door—quiet! Listen. Climb the stove, eat some cereal. Fast. Listen. Chewing. Listen. Chewing. Breakfast of Champions. Hey, let's have a look at the Wheaties guy on this box. This is not Mickey. It's some guy running. Cereal back. Climb down. Unlock the front door, slow. Open the screen, quiet. And I'm out! Down the stairs, running, up the hill, running, and onto the roof where nothing could touch me. 'Til once when I leaped *(He leaps in slow motion)* off the ledge to snare a liner, missed the fire escape and fell three floors. I broke both my kneecaps and had to wear these big metal braces. Couldn't play much after that. They made me honorary ump, though. Let me carry around home plate and call balls and strikes from the roof. But, it was just 'cause I didn't have no legs. I knew that.

Then one night when we couldn't see the ball no more, everybody's dropping down the window well into the laundry room and underground through the buildings. I'm following fast as I can through the boiler room—"Hold up!"—past the porters' apartments—"Wait for me!"—water mains, circuit boxes, zigzagging through the pitch black to these sounds up ahead. And they're all there. Standing. In the dark. Looking down at a girl I've never seen. She's whispering, "Please don't!" but they got her pinned. Taking her clothes off. And I can't move. Can't get the words out. So I turn invisible. Like a dot. But it's TOO BIG! So I run back, back in pitch black with this scream in my head.

Get home, lay in bed, Yankees on, listen to the Redhead in the earplug: "*Ohhh-HO, DOCTOR!!*" But the scream's so big in my head that even The Mick can't get through.

From then on, I go to school, to get somewhere safe. *(He gathers up the baseball cards)* Inside. Anywhere with a book to look in. Stay late in the library studying chemistry and box scores. *(A galaxy appears. He creates an atom using baseball cards)* An atom is the smallest component of all matter. When perfectly complete, it has eight living entities, which we call electrons, surrounding a nucleus. This bears a striking resemblance to our modern-day baseball field! In fact, the game of baseball was created to mirror this, the tiniest particle of life as we know it! The proton in the nucleus is the pitcher on the mound. He holds the atom together and everything revolves around him. Inside him is something invisible, something you can never know. A secret code that can never be broken. The ball and bat are outside forces. The pitcher attempts to keep them apart. If he fails, and the ball is hit into the galaxy, another game begins in another universe far, far away. And it goes on forever. Unless, of course, outside forces intervene. Then you have to go back . . . back to the beginning.

So I ride the trains back and forth listening to the Yankees on my transistor—"He's going back, back, back—" back home when he's asleep and out before he's up. But one morning, I hear the steps, then he's in my room with a bat, standing over me screaming! And I don't know what I did, but it's bad. And I can't move, can't get the words out. And I'm waiting for it, waiting for him to finally hit me. Then I see the Mickey Mantle bat in his hands and I just want him to swing, just want him to hit me out like Mickey would at Yankee Stadium, so I could feel my head fly out of the ballpark, out over the rooftops, out of The Bronx, and not have to think anymore when he's finally going to kill me. *(Lights brighten)* I say, "Hit me." But he don't understand. "HIT ME!" I said. And he stops. 'Cause this voice is coming out of me LOUD, SCREAMING, like HIS voice, and he's scared. And it's like I was him now, like he was me, little, little like me. And he can't touch me! Nobody can touch me! NEVER! NOT EVER! 'CAUSE I AIN'T INVISIBLE!!

As the lights fade to black, baseballs start to fall like rain, building to a torrential downpour.

Cobb

LEE BLESSING

CHARLESTON *(Nodding):* Yup. You and me sure did get around the bases different from the Babe. We had us a Babe Ruth. "The Black Babe Ruth," they called him. Name was Josh Gibson. You remember him. I'm proud to say I played with Josh—managed him, too. That man hit the ball farther than anybody I ever seen, including Ruth. We had a Black Lou Gehrig, too: Buck Leonard. And John Henry Lloyd—he was the Black Honus Wagner. Me, I was the Black Cobb. We didn't get to pick who they compared us to, you understand. Just the man in the white leagues you played most like. Your position, your ability, your temper.

I was a fighter, same as you. Joined the army when I was fifteen. Fought my way through that, then fought my way through baseball. Joined my hometown club, the Indianapolis ABCs. Used to spike a lot of players. Why there was men wouldn't even try to tag me. They'd just step back and let me steal the base. I fought folks all the time. Wasn't just players, neither. I fought umps—hell, one time I punched an owner in the face. On the field, off the field— didn't care where I fought. I hit a man in the shower once, just for throwing a bad pitch in the game. Toughness—that's why I got the name the Black Cobb. That, and hitting over .400 most of the time. It wasn't the worst title, I suppose. It was the only way white people knew me. They never remembered no Oscar Charleston. Just the Black Cobb. Kind of strange, having your fame with another man's name on it.

Cobb

LEE BLESSING

MR. COBB: I was forty-two when I left baseball. I spent the next thirty-three years of my life as someone who couldn't do the one thing that made him special. I could get richer, I could hunt, I could have children I didn't understand, a wife who loved me less and less. I could go to old-timers games, dinners, give interviews. But I could never again . . . feel triumph. My wife Charlie and I bought a retirement home in Atherton, California. We lived there fifteen years, during which she filed four divorce suits. The last one took. The place had seven bedrooms, swimming pool, guest house, servants' quarters, grounds—God, I hated it. Once she was gone, I didn't know what I was supposed to do with myself. I fished, hunted, made more money, gambled, wrote condescending articles about baseball today, got drunk and insulted people, kept a sonofabitch list, sued people, sat, stared. . . . When my cancer came, the only thing that would keep the pain down was a fifty-percent solution of Jack Daniels and milk. And that was me at the end—a sick man shambling around in his robe all day, drinking that. Loneliness is the main road in life—the rest is just a detour. Hell, loneliness isn't even the road. It's the land itself. This country was built on loneliness. It is loneliness.

The Baseball Show

CYNTHIA MERCATI

WOMAN: The last conversation I had with my dad on the day he died was about the Cubs. "Next year," he said, in that low rickety voice, "The Cubs are going to win it all." *(She sits on the edge of the stage)* My dad was an elegant man. It was only when he had that second martini that you could catch signs of the immigrant kid who grew up tough and poor in a tough Chicago neighborhood. When he had that second martini, and when the Cubs were losing, those are the only times I ever heard Dad raise his voice. And if he had that second martini while the Cubs were losing, look out. But I figure he had the right. The Chicago Cubs haven't gone to a World Series since 1945! *(Smiles)* Dad loved me and I knew it, but he was past forty when I was born and very traditional. He couldn't reach into my world, so I reached into his. I took up baseball. But I didn't take up the Cubs. I was twelve and a rebel. *(She stands)* I took up the White Sox! *(And with a flourish, she pulls on the cap)* When I told Dad, he stared at me, straight on. For that instant, I could see the street kid he'd once been. The street fighter you didn't push too far. *(Mimicking the father's voice)* "Don't you know the White Sox once threw the World Series?" Dad asked me. *(In a twelve-year-old's voice)* "At least they were in a World Series to throw!" I shot back. *(Mimicking Dad)* "A White Sox fan in my house. . . ." Dad muttered, but not to me. This, I knew, was addressed to the gods of baseball. *(She sits on the bench)* During the months Dad spent dying, the Cubs won their division. I took my radio, and I went up into my son's tree-house, and I begged the gods to let the Cubs win the playoffs. I thought that'd buy Dad some time. He'd never desert his team in the middle of the Series. *(Beat)* But the Cubs didn't win, and I should have known better. You can't be an American League fan since age twelve and expect the National League gods to listen to you. *(She stands)* My son is a Reds fan. I'm trying not to be angry. *(As if confronting her son)* I'm trying not to say, "A Reds fan? In my house?" Not that I blame him. The Reds have won the World Series in this century! Yeah, it's been easy to be a Reds fan. It's the dry days that come to all of us, people and teams, that will test my son's mettle. *(As the father)* "A fan," Dad used to say after that second martini, "sticks by his team. Even when they're losing, even when they're awful. Even when they're the White Sox." "If you don't stick up for your team," he'd say, "if you don't stick up for your family, your friends, you have no right to expect anyone to stick up for you! If you don't stand up for what you believe in, you don't deserve to have anything to believe." *(Beat)* Dad learned about loyalty in the old neighborhood. They had to have loyalty there. They didn't have much of anything else. He took that loyalty to Wrigley Field and then he taught it to me. I have stuck by my team. I will expect nothing less from my son.

At Dad's funeral, I told the minister I was sure that the gods of baseball were going to miss Dad, but that God, you know, the one who cheers for both leagues, would see to it that he was reunited with those old players he loved so much. I can see Dad now, talking away with all the old Cubs! Gabby Hartnett and Rogers Hornsby and Hack Wilson! They're gonna need eternity to cover all the stats Dad knew!

Bang the Drum Slowly

MARK HARRIS

adapted for the stage by Eric Simonson

DUTCH: Boys . . . Tonight we start shaking these Washington son of a bitches for good. You know . . . to me, they're like a fly buzzing around your head . . . where you sit and watch it for a while without ever raising your hand against it. Like this. *(Dutch watches an imaginary fly)* Bzzzzzz. Go ahead you old Washington fly. Buzz me one more time and I'll snatch you out of the air, and you'll buzz no more. Bzzzz. . . . Bzzzz. . . . Bzzzz goes the fly until you say to yourself, Enough is enough. I have given you over a month now to trail along two and a half and three and three and a half games behind and now I think I will reach up and squash out your miserable life. *(Dutch claps his hands)* Whack! But only one thing is wrong. I look down at my hand . . . and I have no fly. And I think to myself how could I have missed? The fly is still going Bzzzz. Bzzzz. Do you know why I missed the fly? Do you know why the fly is not dead? Do you wish to know? Tell me if you wish to know? Because he flew right through my fingers is why, if you must know, which he should of never done because on paper he was no club a-tall, but only a couple a dozen men and boys dressed up in Washington suits. And if you wish to know why he flew through my fingers, I'll tell you that too. The reason was because my fingers do not work together. The first finger says to the second finger, I do not like you because you won't play cards with me. And the third finger says to the fourth finger, I don't like you from way back. And the next finger says, You should hear what finger number two been saying about you. And the third finger says to the fourth, Leave you and me cut

48

finger number five dead if we see him and tell your goddamn wife to do the same, and bring up your kids likewise. Boys, this is suicide. I seen it happen on other clubs and I was always glad. But it never happens on any club of mine if I can squash it, and by God, I will. Tonight will be the beginning of a new way of things.

Calvinisms

KEN LAZEBNIK

We are in Calvin Griffith's office in the Metrodome, late in the night of June 22, 1984. This is the evening in which he must come to a decision about selling the Minnesota Twins; he weighs his life in baseball against his life in business. Calvin opens the drawer of the desk, gets out some crackers and a can of Cheez-Whiz. He sprays Cheez-Whiz on a cracker. A big gob of it drops on the floor. He looks for something to wipe it up with—can't see anything. Finally, he takes a pack of Twins socks from a give-away night, opens it, and uses a sock to clean up.

CALVIN *(Painfully):* Christ almighty, who'd think I was a catcher? They've taken out so much cartilage. Ah, Jesus, and everything else. I was a pretty damn good catcher. George Washington University. Summers while I was in school I was traveling secretary and treasurer of the Chattanooga farm team. The Lookouts. Uncle sent me there to learn the ropes. In 1937 I became president of that team. I was making $250 a month. At the end of July we were two games out of last place. Our manager was Red Meat Bill Rodgers. Red Meat Bill Rodgers was a crazy man. Son of a bitch ate raw meat. In Birmingham, Alabama, we went to a restaurant together. Nice place. Water-on-the-table, cloth-napkin kind of place. Waitress comes over to take our order, he says, "I'll have a steak just like you got it." "Pardon?" "Just bring me the piece of meat like you got it in the kitchen." So they bring him out a plate with a raw steak on it. The son of a bitch ate a raw steak. I got up—I couldn't stand it. I thought I was going to urp right there. Ever since I can't stand underdone meat. Well done. That's the way to have your steaks. Bill Rodgers would go hunting with us. He'd kill a deer—hang the deer up on a tree, cut the guts out, eat the heart and liver right there. No kidding. Same thing with a bear. *(He starts fishing for more Cheez-Whiz)*

Like I said, the club was two games out of the cellar. It wasn't performing up to our expectations. Uncle let Red Meat go and made me manager. I loved managing. Next year I was president, treasurer, and manager for the Charlotte Hornets and we were headed for the playoffs. Then our catcher, Al Evans, broke a finger, and then so did his sub. Then two more guys caught—and they both broke fingers, too! I'm desperate. "Jimmy," I said, "I know you're an infielder, but we're out of luck. Would you put on the tools of ignorance?" "Yes, sir, coach!" Our pitcher was one of those fellows we got in a Cuban canebrake—Roberto Ortiz. He had an incredible fastball. I mean, it was terrific. And we're in Charlotte with that night ball and those kind of soft lights. Jimmy gets behind the plate. Ortiz winds up. Batter swings. Faint click of the bat—foul ball. Jimmy jumps up, his middle finger is purple and swelling like a balloon. Catcher number five busts his hand. We're out of catchers. I say, "Jimmy, give me that gear." I hadn't caught in six years. I had never played professional ball. But we were in a pennant race, and by God, I was going to keep my team in it! Griffith now catching for Charlotte. I got down and looked up at that big Cuban. He was a huge man. Ortiz threw faster than any man in the league. I flashed one finger. Give me your heat. See what you've got. He went into the big wheelhouse delivery and then—bang—that ball was on me before I knew it. It skidded off my glove and hit the screen behind the plate on the fly. The ball stuck in the wire mesh. I went back to get it. The fans started moving back a couple of rows. I threw the ball back to Ortiz. "Rock and fire, amigo." The next pitch popped into my mitt like a marshmallow. He threw a light ball. And the next day I caught again and got a hit. I kept on catching until Evans' hand healed up. Fellow asked me why did I do it. Call it superstition if you like. All I was trying to do was put the pressure on the jinx. *(Pause. He sprays Cheez-Whiz on a cracker, carefully this time. He eats)*

It's not good for a man of my age to eat alone. Hard on the indigestion system. I know Uncle Clark wouldn't approve of my lifestyle. But he didn't have TV. *(He turns on the TV. Everything's off the air. He clicks it off, gets out vodka and tonic from a desk drawer, pours himself another drink)*

I loved managing. I learned the ways of ball players. I learned how they feel about things and what their problems are. I begged Clark Junior to spend time in the minor leagues but he wouldn't do it. He'd say, "Things are different now." He'd say, "There's no profit in going to the lower minors." You can't learn a ball player's heart from behind a desk, son. All the law and business classes in the world won't tell you why a player's not hitting. No book ever tells you that with a man on first you give the bunt sign. The things you learn on an overnight bus stop, in dingy hamburger stands, on ten-inch planks that are supposed to be dugout benches and dressing rooms in trailers—well, those are things you absorb in your heart. There's no way you can put that learning in a book. You learn the soul of a ball player. Inside every ball player there's a little angel. Sometimes that angel sings every morning and lightens that person's heart and he comes up to the plate with an inner certainty that he's going to connect with the pitch and drive it. It's meant to be, because he can see that ball so clearly, down to the rotation of the stitches, down to the American League stamp rolling over and over in slow motion—that angel inside him is in tune with the heavenly spheres. The sun, the moon, the earth, the ball the pitcher throws—they're all crystal clear. You love to see a player when that angel's singing. He floats along the base, he flies in the green grass of the outfield—he has soft wings inside him. A bad manager is a killer of spirits. He strives with those inner cherubim and fights with them because he wants to run the show, not some godburned ball players.

Now, mind you, some ball players are born without those angels and some are born with devils inside. You've got to find those ones and cast them out. Get 'em out of here. You've got to find men with that spirit inside of them, those bright, quick angels. I don't know how you know, but it ain't rational. After some years of living with ball players on the bus, playing cards, hearing their jokes—you just know which ones got bright angels inside them. Look at that team of '65—what a flock of spirits was in that team. Kitty Kaat, Allison, Earl Battey, Jim Perry, Tony Oliva, the Killebrew. That team floated. You got to love baseball with your heart and soul. You give your soul to it and then it opens up souls to you. You see right through the jersey of men and know their hearts. I don't know exactly how you put together a good ball team, but I can tell you this—it ain't rational.

100 Strikes

KATE MOIRA RYAN

Was I nine when Dad came home with the glove and ball wrapped in plastic? Was Chris still collecting butterflies with his small shirt flying open as his scarred chest and belly button two inches misplaced peeked out? Was my mother sitting outside the field in the park, looking at the broken glass under the green bench remembering when she lost her engagement diamond? I do remember a bat. A Louisville Slugger. Perhaps we had taped it, but I don't think so. I liked how the worn splintered wood calloused my hands. I put the mitt on and gripped hard leather as my right hand traced Nolan Ryan's signature. I cajoled Chris to pick up the bat and hit me one. His scars still pink, he bent down to grab the bat and the ball. We didn't pitch in our sandlot. Pitching broke windows. Pitching meant running after stray balls, wasting time. "How many?" he asked. "How many strikes do I get?" "A hundred," I said. Hoping he would hit one. And so we waited. My mother sitting on the bench. Counting to herself as I bellowed sixty-seven, sixty-eight. . . . I approached the plate several times. "Stand here. Grip the bat like this." I'd walk away towards shortstop as his skinny arms flung and missed. At a hundred we agreed on twenty-five more strikes. My mother said, "Five minutes more. That's it. It's after six." But when the smack of the bat hit the ball, we were well past two hundred. It was a deceiving hit. A pop fly, I thought as I ran under it, but it flew past me. Chris put his hand up to shield his eyes. "Look," he pointed. I turned and ran after the ball, past the first tree, past the big rock, past second base. Finally it descended into the tall uncut grass beyond the second tree. We whacked the grass with the bat and some sticks.

But the birthday ball remained lost. The next spring after the snow melted, I skidded down the little hill of cracking ice, my boot caught a branch, and on the other side of the fence, I saw the ball. I lifted the jagged metal triangle and pulled it out. I found Chris looking for newts under the big rock. I tagged him out. He took the ball from my mittened hands and threw it as far as he could. Past the parking lot into the golf course over the big fence. But we weren't allowed over the big fence. So like Mom's diamond, underneath the green bench, amongst the broken glass, it refused to be found.

The Leap

RICHARD STOCKTON RAND

You need somebody trustworthy to play the roof. Reason is, you can't always see if they catch it on a fly so you've got to trust them on it. Peter Kutnicky, known to his friends as Pricky, was the best I've seen. In fact, I can still see him streaking across a roof to snare a white hardball against a black backdrop of incinerator smoke. He established himself quite a reputation. He even got to the point where he could leap off the roof, catch a line drive in midair, and land on the third-floor fire escape. We called it a "Pricky" in honor of him, and it was something to behold. Like a bird, it was. Except Petey hasn't flown since the last time he hit that fire escape. It was one of those dry Death Valley days in August when nobody in the projects moves more than a mile an hour. Tommy got hold of an inside fastball—prime roof material—and Pricky's gone. Tearing cross the rooftop, leaping skylights, disappearing into a cloud of incinerator smoke, and then he's out over the edge into the thin air where ball meets mitt like it was meant to be. I still see his smile like white neon against red brick. He had it. Then he hit the fire escape and it sliced right off the side of the building. Just hung there dangling over the street making these squeaky metal sounds like it's about to collapse. Poor Petey's just standing there like the guy in the cartoon who realizes he just stepped off a cliff. But this was for real.

It took the ambulance guy two hours to get him out from under the fire escape. They got held up because it was Sunday and they couldn't find a welder to blowtorch a hole through the bars. And Petey wasn't much help squeezing out 'cause he was unconscious most of the time on account of he broke all the bones in his legs. Right before he came to, though, I set the ball in his mitt so he'd think he held onto it. He was proud as hell.

Petey never played much after that, though he still loved the fire escapes. Used to sit on the one outside his bedroom window and watch the games. We even let him call balls and strikes with a pair of binoculars and he loved that 'til one day there was a blowup on a called third strike and Fedorka says, "The only reason you're honorary ump is cause you got no legs." That took all the fun out of it for Petey.

So there ain't much else to say. Except I ran into Petey near Canal Street the other day. We, of course, talked about the catch and he said he still had the ball Tommy hit that day.

"Yeah? I'd kind of like to see it," I told him.

"I'd let you have it for five bucks," he said, trying to be nonchalant. He even offered to sign it for me. Well, I could see he needed the dough so I gave him five bucks and took a look at it, but I couldn't take it.

"Hey, it's your ball now," he says, a little bit offended.

"Nah, are you kidding? I can't take it," and I flipped it to him.

"Okay, well, uh, I'll hang onto it for ya, but it's your ball now. Don't forget."

Then we said "good seeing ya," and took off in opposite directions. I had this feeling, though, that if I turned around just then I'd catch him tossing the ball up and down and I really wanted to see that. So I turn around and there's Petey on the corner showing some guy the ball. He's holding it up like he was Isaac Newton and this ball held the secret to the universe. Then, he hands it to the guy, the guy looks back and forth and then slips something into Petey's palm. Just then, Petey glances down the street and catches me looking at him. I turned and walked away fast. I didn't want to know what was going on. I'm shaking my head now, looking at the

sidewalk and feeling like a walking doofus. I mean, a baseball's just a baseball. And people can't fly. And why can't I get
it through my head that things have changed. For some fucking reason. And it ain't never gonna be like it was.

The Mystery Catcher

STEVE FEFFER

Moe Berg addresses the audience. He is sixty-four years old, and in the last years of his life. He wears a deteriorated version of clothes that once made him look very distinguished and mysterious. His black suit is threadbare, his white shirt badly yellowed, and his fedora is crumpled on his head. For the first part of the monologue, Moe struggles to stand in a posture that suggests his much younger and important self.

MOE BERG: Zurich, December 18, 1944. Werner Heisenberg, the giant of German science, dug in behind the lectern. He arrogantly swung his pointer towards the packed lecture hall like the ferocious Tyrus Raymond Cobb taking a menacing practice cut. It was Heisenberg who'd told a supersect of German scientists that it might be possible to blow up an entire city with a bomb the size of a three-two curveball.

But also in the lecture hall that day, undercover as a mild-mannered physics student, was me, Professor Moe Berg. I had recently completed fifteen seasons of big league ball made memorable by my reputation as the game's brainiest player. It had been written of me that I could speak twelve languages, but couldn't hit a curveball in any of 'em.

On this night I had traded the catcher's tools of ignorance— mitt, mask, and chest protector—for a government-issued forty-five and orders implying that if Heisenberg so much as mentioned the word *atom*, I was to render him *hors de combat.* Or out of the ball game for the less linguistic among you.

Matty's Giants versus Smoky Joe's Sox. Wagner's Bucs versus Cobb's Tigers. Professor Werner Heisenberg versus Professor Moe Berg. The matchup was a classic and the stakes couldn't be higher.

The lights change. Moe's manner more accurately reflects his failing physical and emotional health.

Newark, New Jersey, May 5th, 1970. The tragedy of the world today is that there's no respect for secrets. Everyone wants to know everyone else's business and people are all too happy to oblige. Your secrets are who you are. They are where you most live. I ought to know because I have some doozies. If I didn't, would the United States government have given me one of these? *(Moe takes a pillbox from his suit coat and opens it)*

Government-issued potassium cyanide. *(He snaps the pillbox shut and places a finger to his lips)*

Shhh . . . Not that I *ever* needed it. . . . General Leslie Groves said so himself. "Moe Berg is the last man in the Manhattan Project that needs cyanide to keep from revealing secrets." *(Pause)*

A few weeks ago I was telling a story to an acquaintance of mine. He said to me, "You know, Moe, I don't know all the details, but I'd bet there'd be a lot of publishers who'd pay handsomely for the story of your life. I'd imagine you could get fifty grand easy." "The story of my life?" I said to him. "Now, Irv, you know that isn't me."

Yesterday I get this call. There's a publisher he knows that'd like to talk to me. I say, okay. . . . Fifty grand is fifty grand and what harm can it do to talk? We sit down with this kid that looks like he should be editing his high school sports page, and before we even have our napkins on our laps, the tike says, "Let me tell you, Moe, how much I've enjoyed all your movies." Irv and I look at each other. My movies? What the hell is this kid talking about? Turns out the kid thought that I was Moe from The Three Stooges. Well, Irv turns all red and slams his fist on the table. "Moe from The Three Stooges?!" he hollers. "This is Moe . . . *Berg!* The former catcher for the Boston Red Sox that might've saved a million lives with the work he did during W-W-Two!"

I had to calm him down before he got us thrown out of

the place. "Forget it, Irv," I say, "I don't need this kid. I can do the book myself. It's time for me to do it anyway. Hell, I'll start it as soon as I get home." *(Pause)*

As soon as I sat down at the typewriter I knew I couldn't write it. My secrets are the most important thing in the world to me. They're essentially all that I have left. They are *Professor* Moe Berg. They're the stories I barter for food, drink, and shelter. "Professor Moe Berg on the ball fields of Princeton calling signals in Latin to my teammates." "Professor Berg slipping out of the bullpen in a kimono to take recon photos of Tokyo during an American All-Star tour of Japan." "Professor Berg's courtship of atomic physicist Lise Meitner in an SS-surrounded bungalow." My parlor tricks with philology, baseball trivia, and linguistics.

Once I set down the quote-end-quote definitive account, you'll have no more use for me. But as long as I'm here in Newark and keeping my secrets to myself, Professor Berg is there for the world. I'm there for the world. And, trust me, you need me now more than ever.

(A whisper) You need me now more than ever. Shhhh!

The lights change. Moe slowly tries to return to the vigor of his spy days.

For example, if I hadn't walked to the newsstand this morning, I would've never seen Professor Werner Heisenberg here on the streets of Newark. He was turning down Washington Street carrying a *New York Times* and a briefcase. I was so close to him it was as if it were Zurich in 1944. *(The lights begin to fade. Footsteps are heard. Moe follows them)*

Maybe today's the day he'll say something extraordinary. "Yes, I have an atomic bomb. I have it right here. It's the only one and I'm the only one who knows how to build it." *(The footsteps grow in volume while Moe stays close behind by hiding in the shadows)*

You think you know who I am, but you can't. No one can. A man like myself accepts that. You say that the times have changed, and the work that I did was of a different era, but we both know there's always a premium for it. That's why I'm still doing it. And, you'll see that you've needed me all along. *(The footsteps fade into the darkness)*

In fact, I'm hot on the trail, even as we speak.

Moe takes the pillbox out of his pocket. He opens it and looks in. He pauses for a moment and then returns it to his jacket. Moe brings a finger to his lips and turns toward the audience. In a whisper, he gives them a final "shhh." He turns back away from them and exits into the darkness in pursuit of Heisenberg, who has long since disappeared.

Babe

CYNTHIA L. COOPER

Babe Didrikson seems tall, although she is only five-foot-six. She is angular and has a magnificently athletic body. Her Texas roots show in her voice, as does her homegrown education and a certain kind of naivety mixed with egotism.

BABE: They named me Babe back in Beaumont, Texas. See, one day—around 1920, reckon, when I was about nine—I walked out to the baseball diamond where the boys was playing. *(Babe grabs a bat, motions)*

I picked up one of them bats and signaled the fella that was pitching to throw me a few. He didn't really want to and twisted all around on the mound. Finally he puts one my way. *(She swings, then watches)*

Well, I whacked that ball good. *(Resumes batting position)*

So he comes at me with another. *(She swings, watches, lines up again)* I whacked that ball even harder. Now he winds up and throws me the best pitch he's got. And I whacked that ball the hardest anyone ever had on that field.

"She hits like Babe Ruth," one of the boy called. *(Barely stopping, Babe signals for more pitches)*

"I might hit like Babe Ruth," I said. "But I might hit a whole lot better, too." *(Continues to swing, watch balls being hit a long way)*

I wasn't too much older before I figured something was wrong with Beaumont. Most of the gals was in the Miss Purple Club, which was something designed "to encourage our boys in athletics to victory." I weren't no Miss Purple and no Miss Purple was encouraging me to victory. I left Beaumont. But everywhere I go, whatever game I play, I'm still Babe.

. . . a catcher to his pitcher

JUDY GEBAUER

A bullpen. A veteran catcher and a rookie pitcher [unseen]. The catcher squats, throwing the ball to and receiving it from the "pitcher" offstage.

CATCHER: Don't let them know. Don't let them see it hurts. Just throw easy. They just want you up and throwing. Hurt goes away. Young as you, it goes away. *(Throws ball. Lifts mask and spits)*

Don't sweat it, Rusty. They're gonna call in the right-hander today. They're gonna call Fulargi. Guaranteed. You been watching that mess out there? They don't want to put you in that bag of shit. They got you up to throw for the cameras. Work out that sore muscle. Swear to God, Rusty. Today's not your day. You're in the clear. Toss it for the cameras. *(Catches ball. Stands and prowls about)*

Just get the kink outta my back. Kill a little time for you. That went first. The back. Then the knees. Shit, what a mess they got out there. Call this championship play. Write this one off the books. See, you're the phenom from triple-A, they bring you up now for the pennant race, they gotta show you off. But the skip's not gonna waste you on a mess like this. After the fourth, that six-run joke, it was a washout. We're just going through the motions now. They're not gonna put you in to win it back. They're gonna put you in when you can save something. What's to save out there today? Okay? Shoulder still stiff? *(Squats and throws)*

But the time's gonna come you'll go out. Might as well get used to it. It goes fast. I come up in '78. Here we are. Where'd those years go? Keep it low, kid, you're throwin' a little wild. Not too hard yet. Just nice and easy does it.

(*Back and forth during*) Things I seen behind this mask. Only the phantom knows. I see a guy's wife in the right-field seats and his girlfriend in the left-field seats. Same game. Namin' no names. My roommate '84 season, pitcher, left-hander like you. What a fucked season that was. I had the sweetest season in '83 and then comes '84. For me it was one big slump and sore knees. Got so I had the shakes when I come up to the plate. I couldn't hit. I lost my swing, I lost my feel. I couldn't read the ball comin' in. I'm on the road, now, halfway through this piss-drinking season, me and Jippy, my roommate, this southpaw. So this night in Chicago I say, look, Jip, let's single this stand. I want my own room. Just be alone. Quiet. Early to bed. I need the alone time. So, okay, our room's booked already so I get another one and Jip takes the one reserved for us. Now Kim calls. My wife. Calls me like she always does, gets put through to the room I share with Jippy. Desk mistake, I guess. My name's on that room. So who answers . . . getting wild, kid, keep it down and inside here, just down and inside, just steady for now, no pretty stuff for now . . . okay, who picks up the phone, this girl. . . . Kim asks for me, this girl says I'm not there, the truth, I'm not there. Kim says what's your name, this girl says Diane, Kim says how old are you, this girl says nineteen. Kim's crazed. Hangs up. Never hear word one about this. Okay. Finish the Chicago stand, don't get a fuckin' hit, on to the next stop, back to doubling with Jippy, now Kim calls me, not one thing about Diane. My kid's twelve, his Little League won their division, he goes out and gets drunk. Some kid's big brother got a bottle of red wine. Kim's telling me our boy's sick in bed drinking wine, he's twelve. I'm goin' outta my tree, I'm saying, how'd he get drunk, she's tellin' me to get a grip, his team won, I'm all, so what his team wins, he has to go get drunk! She says to me, you do it when your team wins, I'm all, I'm not twelve fuckin' years old, she's all, he threw it all up, I'm thinking she sounds upset and sad because I should be there with her through this and I'm not, my kid's turning into a drunk and I'm not even

65

there, never a thing about Diane but that's what she was thinking. Come home. Fly in late, it's pouring rain, right, never rains here. Chamber of Commerce goes out of its mind if it rains here, it's a fuckin' deluge, worst since last century. No Kim at the airport. Kim's always there no matter what time. No Kim. So okay. I make a quick call, no Kim, kid's at a friend's overnight. Okay. Catch a ride with Jip and Dumbo and them. Get home. Inside, there's my kid with this Australian guy. Whole neighborhood's dark. Power outage. So my boy got nervous, goes next door where this Aussie guy I never met before lives, gets him to come over. He comes over all the time, so how come I never met him. Okay, so in comes Kim all drenched. Flat tire on the highway on the way to pick me up, which she changes herself thanks to my teaching her how to do that when we first got together. Then she proceeds to make introductions, like Jeff is this Aussie guy, she says Jeff this is . . . and nothing, she can't think of my name, she's staring at me, I mean we've had two kids together, we slept together how many millions of times, she draws a blank, so I have to tell her my name's Jad. I'm that guy she's married to, and then this guy and me shake hands and he goes on home and Jippy and Dum and them go and we got the house to ourselves and I'm thinking this Aussie guy's boffing my wife, and I'm pissed he's in my house looking after my kids, but okay let's hear what Kim has to say. So we hem and haw and she sends the kids on up to bed, and it's still all candles lit and flashlights, and she makes me a cheese sandwich in the candle-light and we break out some beer, Kim says I gotta drink it before it turns warm in the fridge, and then I just say, look, if something's going on around here I shouldn't know don't tell me, just knock it off whatever it is, don't tell me. Kim says there's nothing. The Aussie guy's been a good friend. I know this girl, Rusty, I slept with this woman, I know this woman and this woman is saying to me, I love you baby, and I been lonely and this Aussie guy could've been something but you're the one, and all of a sudden I'm feeling real old and real scared for the first time in my life. I'm too old for this game and I'm gonna be a free agent and I don't know what's gonna happen to me if my season stays in the shit, and if this woman goes I don't know what I'll do. Kim says it hurt her about Diane but she's going noplace. I'm like, Diane? She's, Diane in Chicago. I'm, I don't know any Diane in Chicago. She tells me she phoned me there and Diane answers and I'd stepped out and Diane's nineteen and I'm like, Diane? And then I'm on my third beer and it's all clear. It's Jippy. See, me and Jip in Chicago, he's had women in, me never, and they're not nineteen before and I usually turn on the TV or roll over and ignore it. So Jippy's gone home to Holly and the three daughters and I'm sitting here with Kim finding out about Diane. The lights never do come back on that night and I think we polish off a twelve-pack and do it on the living room rug and it's so good, Rusty, the best, you know, full of beer on the rug, it's so good, and I wake up in the morning, my two babies peeking over me, my little girl says, that's disgusting, and she and her brother go in the kitchen and make cereal. And I go out to the park that afternoon, first home stand back from the road, go out, oh for four, but I'm happy. The Aussie guy's just a good neighbor and Kim's mine for good. But up there in the seats, look through this mask, there's the wives and the girlfriends. And there's Kim and just Kim. *(Back and forth)*

One time I got bases loaded and a heavy hitter at the plate and Jippy hung over on the mound and I'm chewing sixteen wads of bubble gum and making with the remarks, you know, psyche out this muscle at the plate, and I blow this bubble, inside my mask, you know, and it gets all the fuck over the . . . had to call time, stop the game, swear to Jesus I didn't do it to throw the rhythm, just forgot I had on the mask, clean out my mask, gum in my hair, all over my glasses. *(Back and forth)*

And then they bring up somebody from triple-A and you're not playing every day. Then you're platooned. Then you're on the bench. Then you're the bullpen catcher warming up the savers. And then you're. . . . I been with this club my whole big league career. Whole seventeen years same club. Seventeen years I been squatting here. Make the most of your years. *(Back and forth)* Make the most of it. *(Holds onto the ball)*

I broke my leg in '89. That was blocking the plate. That was Conception ran me down. Great player. Good man. Fine man. Plowed right into me. Got these bolts in this knee here. Go through the security gizmo at the airport, hey, hell breaks loose. Carry my X-ray around so I can prove it's only bolts. So don't ask where my blazing speed went. I gotta hit home runs 'cause I can't run like I used to could. I used to could run. Catcher gets old quick. In the back and the legs. *(Silence)*

Was I right or was I right? They're calling in Fulargi. Your day's coming. But it'll be a winning day. When there's something to save. You're the rising star, Rusty. Okay, now let's try the spitter. You got your spitter today? *(Back and forth)*

Guy comes up to me, I'm at Disneyland with the kids, this is last January sometime, I'm in the urinal in Fantasyland, guy comes up, got his own kid with him, says, you guys better do better next season, what's wrong with you guys, don't you guys make enough? I'm standing right there with my dick in my hand, this guy's kid standing right there, he's reaming me about the season. Disneyland. *(Back and forth)*

Lower and inside, Rusty. Don't ever get so you whine. Just go out and do it and that's it for the day. Guy comes up to you in the head, says something shitty, smile. *(Silence)*

Don't they get it? Don't they notice the grand slam you hit bottom of the ninth? How long's a guy's memory for the good stuff? What does he think, I want to go oh for four every day? I work at it? Pretty soon your shoulder goes, like a rotator cuff, your back, your legs. You're thirty-five and you're old. See, Rusty? Don't get so you whine all the time like me. *(Back and forth)*

In '83 I couldn't make a mistake. I couldn't walk but I couldn't make a mistake. A ball didn't get by me. I picked off a hundred guys. They couldn't throw me anything I couldn't hit. It was just that kind of golden time. Scary kinda. Guys in the clubhouse wouldn't talk to me. Scared to jinx me. Press stood around but nobody talked to me. It was lonely but it was gold. That's nice, Rusty, that's sweet. Right like that. Hear how that hit the mitt? That's what you want. How's your change-up? Nobody's looking at you. Try your knuckle-ball. What a sweet surprise that's gonna be, you throw the knuckler. I know just when and just who. They'll look at you then. They're gonna be looking at you plenty pretty soon. You let your catcher walk you through it. Let him think for you, for now anyway. I used to go out to the mound and yell at Inman 'cause he needed the steam. Never yelled at Quint. Not his style. He needed a backrub or a kind word. But Inman, you gotta abuse him, he gets sore, he gets good. So, we'll see what you like, Rusty. They're gonna be watching you for a long time.

Back and forth.
Back and forth.
Back and forth.

Feffer and the Giants Are #1

STEVE FEFFER

STEVE: A. Bartlett Giamatti wrote that baseball is the most eternal of all games because it was designed to despair us. In the spring it arrives bringing us hope, in the summer it blossoms and becomes easy to take for granted, and in the fall—when we need it the most—it's gone.

Six weeks ago my father died of a sudden heart attack at the age of fifty-four. The last time I ever saw him alive was a week and a half before, when he and I attended a late September ball game between our beloved Chicago White Sox and the Detroit Tigers at the old Comiskey Park. It was a meaningless game in the standings, but a game that was made remarkable by a couple of facts: first, my father and I had not attended a baseball game together since 1981, when after attending a hundred or so games in the two decades prior, I went away to college in Boston; and second, the last-place White Sox won, which in 1989 happened a mere sixty-eight other times.

As I think how appropriate it is that a ball park should've been the last place I ever saw my father alive, I'm reminded of a story about him—and my own playing days—the year the West Rogers Park Giants went to the Chicago Little League Playoffs.

The year the Giants went to the playoffs was 1973, and I was eleven years old. First of all, I think it's important to understand that the nickname "Giants" was an incredible misnomer. You see, the West Rogers Street "Giants" were me and the twelve other little Jewish kids who lived in my predominantly Polish and Greek neighborhood. The infield from third to first was Levinson, Cohen, Feffer, and Cohen.

The Cohen brothers, Billy and Steve, making up two thirds of the Giants' legendary double-play combo.

That spring, a remarkable twist of fate happened to the previously hapless and physically inadequate Giants. My mom's best friend, Mrs. Woolf, adopted an eleven-year-old kid of some unknown origin—i.e., not Jewish—who was twice as big and strong as any of the Giants. At that point in my life he was by far the largest eleven-year-old I had ever seen. And since my mom and his mom were friends, I became his first friend, and Brad Woolf was recruited to join the Giants. Needless to say, he was awesome, and the one true giant became our starting and only pitcher, and our cleanup and only hitter.

Behind Brad Woolf, the West Rogers Park Giants made a remarkable turnaround. And we won, no exaggeration, every game the rest of that summer and earned the right to play in the Chicago Little League Playoffs.

This was exciting because it meant our playoff would be held in Thillens Stadium, which is this real baseball stadium in Chicago with stands, a scoreboard, and best of all, real *dugouts*. Yes, *dugouts*. A far cry from the muddy diamonds that were scattered across frequently flooded River Park, where the Giants claimed the pennant.

Unfortunately, on the day of our playoff game at Thillens Stadium, I very quickly learned that there are, in fact, a lot of eleven-year-olds as large as Brad Woolf, and it seemed to me that wherever Mrs. Woolf had adopted Brad, our opponents, from the West Side of the city, had adopted a whole team. They were *giants*. And they all threw as hard as Brad Woolf, they all hit as far, and they were all of some unknown origin, i.e., not Jewish. And as we took the field together for some pregame infield and batting practice, this fact did not go unnoticed by my teammates, who thought it might just be the perfect fall day to stay in one of those really cool dugouts and *watch* a baseball game. One by one, the Giant nine, with the exception, of course, of Brad Woolf, began to fake an

71

assortment of injuries, so that by the time that infield practice was completed there were so many limping Giants dragging bad legs, we resembled a chorus line of Quasimodos in a big production number entitled: "No, coach, I think it's sprained. I just need to sit this one out."

It wasn't until after the national anthem that the Giants got the fire they needed to want to take the field, and it was in anger at me, their starting second baseman. As the umpire shouted, "Play ball," and I returned my hat to my head from its patriotic place across my heart, my dad, who was seated prominently behind home plate, unfurled a banner that read: FEFFER AND THE GIANTS ARE NUMBER ONE. It was the only sign in the ballpark and from where I stood at second base it appeared as if the whole proceedings had suddenly come to a stop so that everyone on the field and in the stands could read this important pronouncement, figure out who the hell Feffer was, and how *he* could possibly make the Giants "number one."

Perhaps at this point it's important to note my contributions to that great Giant team. Because, in fact, I was not "number one," I was number nine. The ninth-place hitter, barely hitting my weight and this during my svelte years. But, I started nonetheless because I was a vacuum in the field. I could really flash some leather. And if you play catch with me after we're done here, you'll see that it's still true. But FEFFER . . . *AND* THE GIANTS. Not quite. . . .

Anyway, my teammates, except for Brad Woolf, responded to the banner by letting loose a stream of profanity and abuse at me that only eleven-year-olds could hurl at a really good friend. And every time my dad held up that sign, it just got worse. When I was up at the plate, my own team yelled, "Hey Batter Batter, miss!" When I called for a pop-up, they'd step in front of me. When the ball was thrown around the horn, they skipped my spot. In short, I should've been devastated.

But, the truth was, I wasn't too bothered. What I couldn't understand was why none of the other fathers of any of the other ball players on that field had made them a banner. And, what I realize now, particularly that he's gone and I miss him so much, is that my father had always been steadfast in his faith in me. He genuinely believed that whether it was writing or playing second base for the Giants that if I worked hard at something, extraordinary occurrences would follow. Such as: the Woolfs would adopt Brad, Brad would play for the team I was on, and we would go to the playoffs.

The Giants lost this game. We got crushed. Not a single hit. Not even Brad Woolf, who also got rocked on the mound. We didn't even have a base runner get farther than first, until:

I came up in the seventh, which is the last inning of a Little League game. And I like to believe that I saw the pitcher look up, see the sign my dad was holding, look in the Giant dugout, and get the okay from my teammates and manager, before rearing back and popping me so hard in the shoulder with a fast ball that I still feel it. Of course, in the majors, there's an unwritten rule that when a pitcher throws at a hitter, he's not supposed to rub it. And in this way the batter doesn't let the hurler know he's got any stuff. Well, I hope I didn't give too much away rolling around in the dirt in agony. I can only hope the pitcher thought it was some unrelated seizure. And in this moment of extreme athletic defeat, my dad came to the screen at the foot of the grandstand, still holding the damn sign, and said, "Rub it off, Fefferman. Rub it off." And I thought to myself, "Rub it off, Dad? Rub it off? I don't think I can find my arm right now to rub it off." And then he said again, "Rub it off, Fefferman, and get to first."

Well, I did. I got to first. And then I did an incredible thing. Down ten to nothing, in the last of the seventh, when we desperately needed base runners, I, the slowest guy on the team, stole second. I don't know what motivated me. But I stole second. I got farther than any other Giant in this game. Including Brad Woolf. My teammates were stunned. The opposition was stunned. My coach was so stunned he came out to second base to ask me if the ball had hit me in the head and not the shoulder. But I was there. On second. And two outs later I was still there, and the ball game was over.

And today, as I write this, I'm thinking of how difficult these past six weeks have been since my dad passed away, and I'm struggling with all the unimaginable things that have happened to me in that short time. It's October, and baseball is leaving me at a time when I need it the most. I see my dad, coming to the front of the bleachers, holding that sign that says FEFFER AND THE GIANTS ARE NUMBER ONE, and he's telling me to rub it off, and get to first base. . . .

The Green Fields
of the Mind

A. BARTLETT GIAMATTI

It breaks your heart. It is designed to break your heart. The game begins in the spring, when everything else begins again, and it blossoms in the summer, filling the afternoons and evenings, and then as soon as the chill rains come, it stops and leaves you to face the fall alone. You count on it, rely on it to buffer the passage of time, to keep the memory of sunlight and high skies alive, and then just when the days are all twilight, when you need it most, it stops. Today, October 2, a Sunday of rain and broken branches and leaf-clogged drains and slick streets, it stopped, and summer was gone.

Somehow, the summer seemed to slip by faster this time. Maybe it wasn't this summer, but all the summers that, in this my fortieth summer, slipped by so fast. There comes a time when every summer will have something of autumn about it. Whatever the reason, it seemed to me that I was investing more and more in baseball, making the game do more of the work that keeps time fat and slow and lazy. I was counting on the game's deep patterns, three strikes, three outs, three times three innings, and its deepest impulse, to go out and back, to leave and to return home, to set the order of the day and to organize the daylight. I wrote a few things this last summer, this summer that did not last, nothing grand but some things, and yet that work was just camouflage. The real activity was done with the radio—not the all-seeing, all-falsifying television—and was the playing of the game in the only place it will last, the enclosed, green field of the mind. There, in that warm, bright place, what the old poet called Mutability does not so quickly come.

But out here on Sunday, October 2, where it rains all day, Dame Mutability never loses. She was in the crowd at Fenway yesterday, a gray day full of bluster and contradiction, when the Red Sox came up in the last of the ninth trailing Baltimore eight–five, while the Yankees, rain-delayed against Detroit, only needing to win one or have Boston lose one to win it all, sat in New York washing down cold cuts with beer and watching the Boston game. Boston had won two, the Yankees had lost two, and suddenly it seemed as if the whole season might go to the last day, or beyond, except here was Boston losing eight–five, while New York sat in its family room and put its feet up. Lynn, both ankles hurting now as they had in July, hits a single down the right-field line. The crowd stirs. It is on its feet. Hobson, third baseman, former Bear Bryant quarterback, strong, quiet, over one hundred RBIs, goes for three breaking balls and is out. The goddess smiles and encourages her agent, a canny journeyman named Nelson Briles.

Now comes a pinch hitter, Bernie Carbo, onetime Rookie of the Year, erratic, quick, a shade too handsome, so laid back he is always, in his soul, stretched out in the tall grass, one arm under his head, watching the clouds and laughing; now he looks over some low stuff unworthy of him and then, uncoiling, sends one out, straight on a right line, over the center-field wall, no cheap Fenway shot, but all of it, the physics as elegant as the arc the ball describes.

New England is on its feet, roaring. The summer will not pass. Roaring, they recall the evening, late and cold, in 1975, the sixth game of the World Series, perhaps the greatest baseball game ever played in the last fifty years, when Carbo, loose and easy, had uncoiled to tie the game that Fisk would win. It is eight–seven, one out, and school will never start, rain will never come, sun will warm the back of your neck forever. Now Bailey, picked up from the National League recently, big arms, heavy gut, experienced, new to the league and the club; he fouls off two and then, checking, tentative, a big man off balance, he pops a soft liner to the first baseman.

It is suddenly darker and later, and the announcer doing the game coast to coast, a New Yorker who works for a New York television station, sounds relieved. His little world, well lit, hot-combed, split-second-timed, had no capacity to absorb this much gritty, grainy, contrary reality.

Cox swings a bat, stretches his long arms, bends his back, the rookie from Pawtucket, who broke in two weeks earlier with a record six straight hits, the kid drafted ahead of Fred Lynn, rangy, smooth, cool. The count runs two and two, Briles is cagey, nothing too good, and Cox swings, the ball beginning toward the mound and then, in a jaunty, wayward dance, skipping past Briles, feinting to the right, skimming the last of the grass, finding the dirt, moving now like some small, purposeful marine creature negotiating the green deep, easily avoiding the jagged rock of second base, traveling steady and straight now out into the dark, silent recesses of center field.

The aisles are jammed, the place is on its feet, the wrappers, the programs, the Coke cups and peanut shells, the detritus of an afternoon; the anxieties, the things that have to be done tomorrow, the regrets about yesterday, the accumulation of a summer, all forgotten, while hope, the anchor, bites and takes hold where a moment before it seemed we would be swept out with the tide. Rice is up, Rice who Aaron had said was the only one he'd seen with the ability to break his records, Rice the best clutch hitter on the club, with the best slugging percentage in the league, Rice so quick and strong he once checked his swing halfway through and snapped the bat in two, Rice the Hammer of God sent to scourge the Yankees, the sound was overwhelming, fathers pounded their sons on the back, cars pulled off the road, households froze, New England exulted in its blessedness, and roared its thanks for all good things, for Rice and for a summer stretching halfway through October. Briles threw, Rice swung, and it was over. One pitch, a fly to center, and it stopped. Summer died in New England and like rain sliding off a roof, the crowd slipped out of Fenway, quickly, with only a steady murmur of concern for the drive ahead remaining of the roar. Mutability had turned the seasons and translated hope to memory once again. And once again, she had used baseball, our best invention to stay change, to bring change on. That is why it breaks my heart, that game—not because in New York they could win because Boston lost; in that, there is a rough justice, and a reminder to the Yankees of how slight and fragile are the circumstances that exalt one group of human beings over another. It breaks my heart because it was meant to foster in me again the illusion that there was something abiding, some pattern and some impulse that could come together to make a reality that would resist the corrosion; and because after it had fostered again that most hungered-for illusion, the game was meant to stop, and betray precisely what it promised.

Of course, there are those who learn after the first few times. They grow out of sports. And there are others who were born with the wisdom to know that nothing lasts. These are the truly tough among us, the ones who can live without illusion or without even the hope of illusion. I am not that grown-up or up-to-date. I am a simpler creature, tied to more primitive patterns and cycles. I need to think something lasts forever, and it might as well be that state of being that is a game; it might as well be that, in a green field, in the sun.

The Umpire

LARRY GERLACH
From *The Men in Blue*

BEANS REARDON: People think an umpire stands out there just waiting for a player to kick so he can send him to the showers. What we really try to do is call them so nobody can argue. The best umpire is the guy who has the least arguments, and runs the ball game, and gets along with the boys on both clubs. Players, managers, and owners don't want a guy who can't run his business without a lot of fuss.

You can't allow the players to take control of the game. You've got to lay down the law. When guys get out of hand, you just show them that your job is to run the ball game and that you're going to run it. You don't go looking for anybody. That's bad. You give everybody an even break. You don't have to chase too many. Ball players are fighting for the pennant, so they don't want to get chased. Once they know you'll run them, they'll behave. They learn real quick.

The main thing an umpire has to do is to make the ball players respect you. You do that by controlling the game. I let them know when I walked on that ball field that I was in charge, and if they didn't like it, I'd give them a ticket out of there. There are lots of ways to convey the message. Sometimes I'd go out on the field and a guy would say, "Hey, Beans, old boy, how's everything?" I wouldn't answer, so they'd say, "Look out, he's mad today." Sometimes, before a tough series or after the home team had given us a rough time the day before, I'd meet with the managers at home plate before the game and say, "Just a minute. Go back to your bench and tell them I'm not taking any kicks today. The first son of a bitch who opens his mouth is gone. I'm going to keep this game under control today." Hell, they can't say anything. It's like arguing with a policeman. You've got the authority like the policeman on the beat. If they don't do what you tell them, you run them.

I was always a hustler. I was small and quick and always tried to be right on top of plays. You couldn't get there all the time, but if you hustled, the players would give you credit for it. You just had to hustle. In any line of work you have to hustle, you have to work. You can't sit down and relax and say, "Well, bring it to me." Hell, no. You gotta go get it if you want it.

We worked with three men in those days. Never had four unless it was an All-Star or World Series game. It was tough for two men to cover the bases. Sometimes you couldn't get over there fast enough to make the call; sometimes you could get blocked out of the play. When that happened, you just had to guess at the play. I know damned well I had to guess at a few. If I was wrong, I caught hell; if I was right, they never said anything, that's all. Today with four umpires it's a much different situation because they're in better position.

Beans Reardon missed some—maybe called plenty of them wrong. Naturally it bothered me when I kicked one because I didn't want to do anything to hurt a guy. I just wanted to run the game and give them the best I had. But once a decision has gone wild, the damage has been done, and no amount of arguing can change it. When the play is over, you've got to forget it—right or wrong. It would be fatal otherwise.

When you see an umpire answer a player's squawk before the player can get it out of his mouth, you know the umpire knows he is right and is willing to go ten rounds. But if you see an umpire backing away and acting like he wasn't invited to the party, it's a sure sign that he is admitting to himself that he might have missed one.

The ball players never bothered me. A little talk now and then is all in a day's work. But the bird in the stands who starts riding you real good can sometimes wear a sore spot.

Yeah, the crowd bothered me. Some guys say you don't pay any attention. That's a lot of bull. The crowd can get on you, make no mistake about that. You'd have fifty thousand people in the stands, and forty-nine thousand would be against you. Naturally it makes you mad when they're calling you names. But there's no way you can get back at them. The only way would be to be crooked and call plays against the home team, but you couldn't do that.

Nobody likes to be hollered at. You can't do anything with the people in the stands; you've got to take it out on the players. If the fans are hollering and some guy picks it up and gets obnoxious, you knock him off and let him know who the hell is the boss out there. But mostly I figured: what the hell, let them yell. It's an aggravating thing, but if the crowd's going to hurt you, you might as well quit because you're going to be in trouble all the time.

Pittsburgh and Philadelphia had the worst fans in the league. They were pretty crazy over in Brooklyn, too, but they were fun. The whole damned Brooklyn Sym-Phonie would give us "Three Blind Mice" when we walked on the field. The organist, Gladys Goodding, started that. You can't play it in ballparks anymore; I complained to the Brooklyn club and they put a stop to it. That Hilda Chester was something. She'd sit there in Ebbets Field ringing that bell and yelling at the umps all the time. One time I asked her what she yelled at us. She said, "Open your other eye, joik; you got noive like a toothache."

Anyway, Larry Goetz hated the hollering. And it ate up Babe Pinelli. Me? Hell, I thought it was fun. I'd ignore them or growl back at them. The fans got a kick out of it when I'd growl at them.

The only time fans like umpires is on a rainy day. The ball players don't want to play, of course, but the fans want to see the game, so we'd get a big hand when we walked out on that wet field. It was like music to my ears. Of course, they'd boo the hell out of your first call.

I like that rule about not selling beer in bottles in the ballpark. In my day, bottles would come flying out of the stands. They should never have let fans have bottles—it was like putting weapons in the hands of imbeciles.

It's hard to say what was the most difficult call for me to make. A late, high tag on a slide is tough because you know the crowd is not going to agree with you. But I guess the most difficult call for me was the three-and-two pitch with men on bases when the batter takes a pitch that just nicked the plate so you have to give him the old out sign. That's such an important pitch, you really have to bear down so you don't take the bat out of his hands.

They used to call me old three-and-two. Early in my career I called a guy out at the Polo Grounds on strikes. He looked at me so surprised and said, "I'm not out, Beans. It's only the second strike." I told him, "No, that was the third strike." He was upset. "If I'd have known that, I wouldn't have taken it because it was a real good pitch." Well, I said to myself, nobody else will ever forget it. From that time on I made it a point to say, "Three and two now," or, "Two strikes now," or something like that to let the batter know he had only one more strike coming.

Working the plate is rough. I didn't like it, but I had to do it to keep my job. It's the hottest place in the park. You have to call about two hundred and fifty decisions a day with the sun beating down on the back of your neck and nobody to hand you a sponge and no time in the dugout. You can't fool around back there. You just have to take a little pride in your work back of the bat. When the catcher says, "Nice going. You didn't miss a pitch all day"—well, then you're a pretty big shot.

Throw 'Em Smoke

MARGARET HUNT AND DICK HOLODY

The time is late August 1965. It is the second game of a double-header, which has gone into its twelfth inning, and is still tied. The place is the bull pen. Perry Gladstone is twenty-seven, a starting pitcher who has been ineffective this season. The team still believes he has "smoke," but must develop another "out-pitch." He has not pitched a game in nine days. He knows he'll be cut if he can't come up with something to make him look like a winner. Perry's team is at bat, with one out and a man on third. A hotshot rookie named Kelly is at the plate.

PERRY: Jesus God, Kelly, step into the friggin' batter's box! It's friggin' nine o'clock! Kelly—No! Here we go again. Step out, grab your cap, pull up your pants, yank your cup, tap your cleats, scratch your ass. You're a Human Rain Delay.

I WANNA GO HOME! Hate friggin' doubleheaders. What you say, Ernie? "Let's play two!" Swell. If they let you play, Ernie old man. But if they're petrified to put the ball in your hand, it ain't "Let's play two." It's "Let's watch two." For eight friggin' hours! Let's be reminded twice in one day how friggin' dead your friggin' career is—

Kelly! It's simple. Just hit one out of the *infield*. Run scores. We hold. We go home. Simple. Come on. Hit it out of the—Aw, fuck! Out of the infield and *fair!* Here we go again. Step out, grab your cap, pull up your pants, yank your cup, tap your cleats, scratch your ass. Jesus God!

So, Ernie. Know what I do when we play a doubleheader these days? I get to watch all the hotshot rookies strike out the side. And then FOR TWENTY-TWO FRIGGIN' INNINGS, I get to hear how Espo's gonna get laid after the second game. *(Looks into Espo's open bag. Takes out a small jar)*

He's got KY stashed everywhere. Buys it by the friggin'
case. Helluva bull-pen catcher Espo. Hates pitchers. Specially
starters on the skids. Specially me. Stinkin' up his bull pen.
Maybe I'll be a bull-pen catcher after they cut me—when?
. . . Next time I lose. . . . Nah. I'll be the coach. Like
Orville. I'd be a helluva bull-pen coach. How smart you have
to be to say, "Make 'em beat you, don't beat yourself. Pitch
around the big guy, throw 'em smoke."

Throw 'em smoke. Six years in the minors, two and change
up here, what, twelve pitching coaches? Throw 'em smoke.
Yeah, sure. Whaddaya do when your smoke don't smoke, your
curve don't curve, and your fork ball is all forked up.

I need a pitch. I need a pitch! Kelly goes oh-fer-friggin'-
fifty and gets eighty thousand dollars. The Human Rain
Delay. He still bats cleanup. They're sellin' friggin' posters of
him scratching his butt. The shit I'd get if I tried that! Touch
my cap, pull the bill down, touch my shirt, my sleeve, my
back pocket—five hundred times! They'd say, hey, he's loadin'
the friggin' ball—

Do it, KELLY! *Now.* Just hit it outta the inf—Shit! Now
you decide you ain't a free swinger? NOW? After twenty-two
friggin' innings, with you going oh-fer-friggin'-what?—eight?
Now you get friggin' selective? Aw, Jesus God. Outta the box,
touch the hat, pull up the pants, pull your pud, scratch your
balls, wave your willie to the fifteen fans too drunk to go
home. *(Yelling)* HEY! KELLY! Just hit it outta the—aw, shit!
Eighty thousand for a friggin' double play! *(He looks, realizes
Orville is signaling him. He drops the KY jelly jar)*

Jesus, Orville! You scared me. Nobody's friggin' talked to
me in two friggin' weeks. . . . Rested? I ain't worked in nine
days! . . . You want *me?* . . . So why's Horrigan walking
out—Oh, yeah, if they don't score. . . . *(Laughs)* Jesus God,
Orv—Yeah, sure, sure. *(To himself)* When the game don't
mean squat, I'm your man.

*(He then speaks to himself as Orville, much tougher, much
more Southern, twice as old as Perry)* Gotta protect Horrigan.

Cain't waste *him* in a stupid-ass game like this one. If they don't score, you go in the bottom of the fourteenth. Right. Orville. Why waste hotshot Horrigan when I'm just standing here waiting to be wasted? *(He starts throwing lightly, looks over his shoulder at the game on the field)*

Come on, Rookie. Hang that friggin' curve. You Micky Finn, Guinness breath, small-dicked hotshot. One measly gopher ball NOW, and we all go home! Espo gets laid, the cops beat up the drunks, and I don't get cut. It's so friggin' late it won't even make the morning papers. Your ma won't even know about it. So you get an L. You can afford it. You're six-and-oh. I'm oh-and-four. They put me in, I'm another mile closer to . . . what? Triple-A? Double-A? Coaching high school baseball? Bet you gotta have a diploma to teach high—

Jesus God! Eight pitches, the kid retires the side. So I'm going in. Face the top of the order. Piece a cake, Jake. *(He starts throwing again)* Okay, concentrate, warm up for real now. Shit, I need a pitch. Fucking Espo's throwing it back harder than I'm throwing it to him. *(To Espo)* Smoke this time, Espo! *(To himself)* Shit, he catches it with his bare hands. *(To Espo)* Don't show me up, you friggin' prosciutto hands.

'Course, on the other hand, who cares tonight? Even the drunks wanna go home. Even the umps wanna get laid— Jesus God, we're rallying! Two walks and a hit batter. That's power! *(Laughs)* Christ, their tenth pitcher's worse than me. I'm going in with a lead? WHAT THE—Yeah, Orville, I figured that out. I could get a w—*(He sees the jar of KY, picks it up again)* Espo, you horny bastard, my horny savior. *(He does a ritual before throwing the next practice pitch, elaborate but smooth)* Nothing's friggin' wrong with me, Espo. This is the way I pitch. *(He repeats ritual)* From now on.

Anybody asks, I'm working on my friggin' mechanics just like my coach told me. They check me, they don't find nothin'. " 'Cause there ain't nothin' to find, Ump!" Nothin'—and look at that, we pop up. So, if I hold 'em this inning—

JESUS GOD! But if I don't hold 'em, I gotta stay in—I'm the only—if they stop me, if I get frisked, come clean. Between innings, dab a little KY—where? WHERE?—I know! Wherever they frisked me before!

Yeah, Espo, I hear you. This is my chance. Show 'em I can throw smoke. This is my chance. Throw 'em spit.

Great Expectations

THOMAS G. WAITES

A man in his early forties with a sad face holds a baseball glove while watching TV.

JAMES: I love to watch baseball. Especially this time of year. The World Series. October. The air; the excitement. It brings back memories.

Did I ever play baseball?

Sure. Sure I did.

I played as a kid, son.

I was a second baseman and a shortstop.

How can I ever forget? Meenen Oil versus York Pharmacy. We were in third place and York was in first. I had a hard time learning baseball. I couldn't hit very well because I found out later I was nearsighted. My family was extremely poor and the idea of glasses (let alone an eye checkup) was positively out of the question. However, I did have a thing which no one else possessed and that was the great capacity, at the tender young age of eleven, to copy.

Larry Wolf, the leading pitcher for York Pharmacy, was a guy in my neighborhood and he had an extraordinary pitching arm. The guy was a mini Nolan Ryan. Larry Wolf was an excellent Little League pitcher. He created enough hype for even the Olympic scouts to come and check him out.

I played shortstop. Then I played second base, like I said, but I always wanted to be like Gregg Maddox or Steve Carlton. I was too small at eleven years old to play much of anything else, but I came to practice every single day—like a dog, I never missed a meal. I was strong, and I got a lot out of sports.

"Hey, you guys, look at my forearms. Look at all the veins popping out of my forearm! See how strong I am?" The coach, Mr. Tangelino, said, "Alls that means is you got a lot of blood." Well, that quit me bragging. I used to listen so well to what Mr. Tangelino said at practice that I memorized it. But the kids made fun of me. They called me Mister-Know-It-All. And I was, too. I knew it all. I knew the inner-most thoughts and secrets of Baseball according to Mr. Tangelino and, more importantly, I could recite them.

I wanted to pitch. So I practiced with my boyhood friend named Frog. He was named Frog primarily because of his skin. He was truly the ugliest twelve-year-old on the planet. He was uglier than a lousy maggot-ridden husk of an animal. He was named Frog because he had so many pimples that his face—I mean pimples, whiteheads and blackheads, and they were all oozing at times when you looked at him. He was a heavy kid with dark black-rimmed glasses like Superman, and Frog smoked Salems steadily. I mean, he was so ugly even his mother didn't want him.

Frog and me at the baseball field. Meenen Oil's home field where we practiced. Got the Frogman to come and have a catch with me. I pitched. Got Frog to catch and it was cool. I copied Larry Wolf till I got it perfectly. Then, it was Frogman's turn to pitch.

Frog wound up. He was a lefty. He was angry. He had been beaten by his stepfather a lot. He was crazy about his mother. He throws. It comes in fast. OUCH! My nose. I am in black. I am out. He copied me. They way I copied Larry Wolf, but only better. Frog broke my nose. I wasn't prepared for his speed. The power of the ball from his left arm. It knocked me cold. Woke up in the hot summer sun—knocked completely cold. Out. "My mother's gone kill me," I said when I finally came to.

I never actually told my mom or dad. I just snuck quietly in at dinnertime. Seven ravenous children and an over-worked, tired dad, all trying to eat. Not a pretty sight. Still, I never gave up on my ability to pitch. I watched and practiced and waited. And watched and practiced and waited till I could copy—even after my broken nose—completely copy Larry Wolf.

"Coach. Mr. Tangelino. Could. I uh try pitching?"

Pitching in practice. This was it. My big chance. I wound up. I slashed my fingers across the threads of the new white practice ball. I reached back and kicked up my left leg and at the same time, kicking off of my right leg with all my might and twisting my wrist just like Larry Wolf and throwing side-armed like him. I struck out my first batter and Mr. Tangelino told him to stay up there for a second three strikes. I felt good. I struck him out again. Then a scum bucket from my corner named Charlie Smith was up next. I stared that mother down. I hated him and he always hated me right back. I wound up. I threw. The same pitch I threw to the other guy. The same exact pitch. Then he swung. Like a dumb shit; and the thing broke right before the plate. It was wizardry. It broke up to the left 'cause Smitty was a righty, then it broke out, like. Way out. Like way, far outside of the plate; then, at the last second it would break right across the plate and the fucking batter would swing. Smitty went down in four pitches. And then nobody could hit me. Everybody started talking about me like I was important.

Coach says, "Hey, you, Jimmy Tate? You start Saturday against York Pharmacy." I couldn't believe it. Me. The guy that people used to call Mister-Know-It-All.

I was starting against the first-place team. York Pharmacy. With their purple and gray woollen uniforms. The uniforms of winners. While we had cheap Meenen Oil green, caps with, sort of, nice stripes going down the side. But it wasn't purple. No sir. It wasn't Larry Wolf and the first-place Little League equivalent to the Dallas Cowboys, it was just us. And I was scared. I was staring at defeat. I was staring at victory.

I came home and told my mom. My dad too. I told him and told him and told him again. And finally one afternoon he wasn't working, which was rare, and I asked him—okay, I fucking cornered him—then he talked to me. He was as afraid of me as I was of him. I talked him into having a catch with me. He agreed and we went out the same door to my backyard, into the small, fenced-in, overgrown garbage disposal filled with tires and truck parts and chassis and grease everywhere. My Dad was a mechanic. He often worked three or four jobs at the same time.

I was gonna show him.

I finally had my chance.

I wound up.

I threw really hard and it was a small, maybe twenty-five-foot throw across my backyard, but I put all my stuff on it at once and BLAM! It hit my dad right in the nuts.

A week went by and it was now Saturday. Big game day. After I hit my dad in the nuts with my Larry Wolf curveball, I decided to stop practicing for a while. At least till the game. Bad move. All my life has been a series of attempts to get my father's attention. So I invited my dad to come and watch me start against York Pharmacy. He came. I go out onto the mound. I smell the bleach my mom used on my white uniform pants with the thick green stripe down the sides and the big white buttons on my fly. The uniform felt too big and my hat was so new and green; I felt awkward and silly. Why had I asked him to come to my stupid game. I wasn't going to be any good. My coach, Mr. Tangelino, came out to the mound and handed me the game ball. It was white and new and hard like the first practice ball I threw, but I shrugged off the good-luck charm and I grabbed onto that ball and, as my coach walked away, I wound up and threw as hard as I could.

It didn't go anywhere near the catcher. It hit the backstop. The catcher couldn't even get to it. I threw again.

I hit the backstop again. The catcher looked at me and I looked at my dad, and I tried again. My dad crossed his arms over his tight, maroon, Ban-Lon shirt and shifted his weight from one side to the other. I finally finished my warm-up by finally hitting the catcher in the glove. But my curve wasn't breaking. The first guy came up. A tall skinny blond-haired kid, his team kept yelling, "C'mon Harry, let's get a hit!" So I guess he was Harry and he played first base because I'd seen him before.

I wind up. I pitch.

"Ball one." The ump had a scream like you never heard before.

"BALL TWO." I was really sweating and nervous. I looked to my dad. I think he looked back.

"BALL THREE." Now I was asking for God's help. You know you are in trouble then.

"BALL FOUR."

I walked him. Okay. Calm down. Get yourself together. The coach looks at me like trying to understand why I am so different than the confident Cy Young candidate who pitched in practice. I wanted my dad. Don't you understand that?

The next batter was none other than Larry Wolf himself. The greatest pitcher in Little League was also their number-two hitter. It was humiliating. Larry could tell I was feebly trying to impersonate him. I was not real. I was a fucking copycat. I had no original ideas of my own. So Larry—who was also very homely as a kid (I don't know how he turned out as an adult) but he had a dog face with freckles around his big fat nose and a buzz haircut and a hugely fat butt that really didn't seem to be part of him—adjusted his helmet and raised the bat behind his head. I looked at him hard and sharply. He was a stupid moron, I thought to myself, but he was a tremendous athlete. Not like me. Larry didn't smoke Marlboros or drink beer on weekends like I did; he was a good boy.

I walked him. I walked the next batter and then the next. So as you can figure, I walked in a run and then a second one. Before I had a chance to walk the third run in with no outs, I looked out of the corner of my eye and saw my dad walking away. I just watched him till he became a speck in the distance.

"PLAY BALL," the ump yelled. I saw my dad disappear.

I walked in the third run and my coach pulled me out of the game.

I sat on the bench.

I think I cried. I can't remember.

A Ghost of a Chance

JEFFERY SCOTT ELWELL

Three A.M. The shower in the visiting team's locker room. The room is empty except for Lucky, sitting on the floor of the shower, drinking a beer. Spread out all around him are what remains of a six-pack. Jack appears. By now, Lucky doesn't react to Jack's sudden appearances and continues drinking as Jack speaks.

JACK: Look, it's not your fucking fault! It's my fault, okay. I'm the one who brought it on myself and I'm the one who's got to deal with the fact that I'm dead. So beating yourself up or drinking yourself to death ain't gonna bring me back and it ain't gonna get this team to the Series. *(Looks down at Lucky)*

   I know. If anybody knows, it's me. I'm the best backstop in the majors. *(Lucky looks up at him)* Okay, okay, in the National League. And you're . . . you were . . . the best pitcher . . . and after thirteen years of dicking around on fourth- and fifth-place clubs, we've finally got a team that can go all the way and what do I do? Imagine, the Cubs in the Series. No way. All of Chicago would riot. They'd be carrying us up and down the entire fucking town. We'd never have to work again, not in Chi-town. And what do I do, miserable fuck that I am? Fucking kill myself. Not suicide. No. That would be honorable. That would have some dignity. No, not Jack, not me. I fucking die chasing pussy. I've got a great wife, and a beautiful kid and I'm out at three A.M. with a couple of morons masquerading as teammates and I . . . *(Regaining his composure)*

   I blow it. I blew it, pal. And I don't want you . . . I don't want you to blow it, L. It's too late for me. The only thing I'm good for is . . . shit . . . I don't know what I'm good for

. . . (Tries to grab a can of beer but it falls onto the shower floor) I can't even have a beer . . . no beer, no baseball, no Bren . . . Bren. . . . *(Jack begins sobbing. Lucky looks up at him, sees him crying, and struggles to his feet. He embraces Jack and whispers something in his ear. Jack pulls slightly away, regains his composure again, and looks at Lucky)*

Don't win it for me. I'm not some angel trying to get my wings. I'm no Gipper that you punks need to win it for. Win it for you, L. You, not me. Remember rookie league? You and me, roomies, telling everybody we saw who was on the way down that it wouldn't happen to us. Not us. Not Jack and the L Train. We weren't gonna be slugs. Also-rans. We were gonna make it. We were gonna get to the Series. Win it. Grab the rings, the girls, the endorsements; we were gonna be set for life. That was twenty years ago, L. Now look at us. I'm dead and you're on your way to becoming a charter member of AA. I don't think that's how you want them to remember you, pal. I know it's not how I want to remember you. Not the L Train. Win it for you. No one else. Just you. *(Jack turns away from Lucky and disappears)*

Spit!

JOAN PUMA

Spitting in Pop's monologue is intended to be an effect of language cadence. Dry spitting is highly recommended. "Paradise" by Sade plays before and as the house lights go down. Lights come up on a big blown-up photo/painting backdrop/curtain of a ballpark—the view you get from the top of an entrance ramp, when you get your first glimpse of the diamond, green and glistening and magical—that fills as much of the stage as possible. Pop, dressed in a baseball uniform, enters in front of the photo/painting, looking back at his offstage players calling encouragements and clapping his hands in coach-style triads of claps. He stops a beat downstage right of center, his hands clasped behind his back, maybe rocks slightly on his heels during the following speech. He occasionally paces, à la George C. Scott in Patton.

POP *(Spits, addresses audience):* Now, whoa, there. Sit back down. *(Spits)*

You just sit back down. I don't want ya to be put off. *(Spits)*

But let's face it. I mean, hey. *(Spits)*

It's a natural bodily function. *(Spits)*

See? Nothin' happened. Nothin' happened. It don't hurt no *body*, it's harmless. *(Spits)*

Harmless, natural spittle. We've gotten so couth and prissy nowadays, it's like we can't handle our own bodies. Don't worry; don't worry. I'm not gonna scratch my groin like those big-money boys do on TV. I'm just a-gonna spit. *(Spits, then pretends to be a delicate flower)*

"Oooooh! Spit! How gross!" some of you may be thinking, saying. But what the hell? It's a *natchural* thing. Purfectly natchural by gosh. I mean, what about murder? Starvation? Dishonesty? That's *(Spits)* gross. And what about acid rain? What kind of clean and natural spring water are they gonna find to brew beer with? If you think about it, spit looks pretty good. No acid rain, no nuclear-waste leakeage, no hospital-waste-syringed beach contamination. No way, none of it! This here's clean and natchural stuff, clean and natchural spittle. And, hey! Wait a minute! If you're a-thinkin' what I'm thinkin' you might be thinkin'—I don't *chew* or *nothin'!* This here's pure unadulterated saliva. Lordie, you see blood and guts and immorality left and right on television—to music, no less! *(Spits)*

Don't worry, I ain't gonna pass it around or anything. *(Spits; paces a few beats)*

Now, what I got here is a bunch of kids—seventeen or so of 'em. And I gotta make men of them. Wal, ackshully, *they* gotta make men of themselves. I mean, take the sitiation here. It's the last game of the season. It's the last game of the franchise. The last game and the last season. *(A beat)* We're sixteen and sixty, fer Chrissakes! *(A beat)* And I got seventeen kids! Now, do they want to go out on an upbeat note and win this game, or don't they care? *(Spits)*

Are they going to ackshully *do* something out there, or will they just go limp like milky-toasts. *(Paces a beat)*

Ackshully, it's like this *every* game with these kids. *(Stops; looks around)*

Wind's pickin' up. *(Back to harangue)* They're out there on the field, and I'm in the dugout making the calls, the calls as to whether or not they ackshully *(Spits)* rise above their insipidness. Become men. I check out whether or not they *(Pause)*, whether or not they retain their *(Pause)*, their humanity. Retain? Humph! *Get* it's more like it. What is their humanity? Hell's bells, I'll be damned if I know. *(Paces)*

I do know what's important. What's important? How the hell do I know? *(Paces)*

I don't know, damnit, I just do. It's a feeling, you know? *(Paces)*

What's important? Shit. *(Paces)*

Naming your car—if you got a car. Yeah, that's important. *(Paces)*

Smiling at people. *(Stops)*

Smells like a storm comin'. *(Back to harangue)* What else? Oh, yeah, what's important. *(Paces)*

Sideburns. Yup, sideburns. I mean, do we want a society of skinheads? *(Paces)*

Sissy stockbrokers walking around looking like Gestapo Youth? *(Paces)*

Sitting on fuschia padded toilet seats? *(Paces)*

I get sick when I think of what we've come to, all right. *(Paces)*

Might as well shave off our brains, too. Already shaved off our hearts and souls. *(Hands on hips, thinking; long pause, looks around the audience, slowly)*

Aw, shit!

Pop exits, looking at sky, taking cap off and scratching his head.

Spit!

JOAN PUMA

MARIANNE MOORE:

> Fanaticism? No. Writing is exciting
> and baseball is like writing.

Hello. I'm Marianne Moore. I wrote those lines in 195—um, 50—umm . . . uh . . . the Dodgers were still in Brooklyn . . . or were they? . . . Well, it doesn't matter when. I mean, I've been dead for nearly twenty years. *(A little off track, pats her hair in place)* Now. Up and in, down and away. Indeed! What is it? Or, more to the point, who cares? Well, lucky for you, I do. If it weren't for Pop, and me, and countless others walking around, practicing, um, evangelical zeal, you might all be out there flinging yourselves off bluffs like lemmings right now. Of course, for all anyone really knows *(Further off track)* we might all be doing that very thing right now anyway, but I don't think we are. *(Back to earth)* Oh. *(Pats her hair, calls stage right)* Okay, boys. *(Sid and Jed, batter and catcher, enter, tip their caps, lay down a home plate, and take their stances at it. A beat. M.M. looks up, calls melodically)*

Oh, bo-oys. *(A pointer is lowered; M.M. takes it, goes over and adjusts Jed's arm)*

Hello, there. How long you been playing semipro ball? Seven years? My, that's impressive. You must really love the game. *(Jed raises his mask, gives her a look behind her back, lowers mask)*

Ah, yes. The game. Yes. Up and in, down and away. Oh, *yes!* Well, this *(Points to center of catcher's mitt)* is probably where you think you should throw the ball to have it called a strike. It's the very center of the strike zone. *(Points and circles area from letters on Sid's uniform to his knees) This* is the strike zone. *(Stops; looks Sid over; starts losing it)* Hi. Come here often? *(Shakes herself back to earth)*

Ooph! The uniforms weren't this, ah, form fitting, in my day. . . . Oh, yes. The strike zone usually includes anything thrown—any ball, that is, thrown—between *(Points)* the letters and the knees and within the imaginary vertical lines that stand for the horizontal boundaries of the plate, home plate—*(Points a line around home plate and in the air to indicate the corners)* the *corners* of the plate. I say usually, because all strike calls—therefore all strikes—are governed by the umpires. *(Looks around to see if audience is following this)* You know, the guys in dark blue suits or light blue short-sleeved shirts and masks who lean over or semicrouch behind the catcher? Now there are a sizable number of these umpires who consider themselves to be sighted even though they are not. But I digress.

The point of true baseball is to strike out the batter. *(Sid straightens and turns toward her, hands on hips)*

Now you may have thought that the point of baseball is to hit the ball, but that's hogwash, sissy baseball. Most folks don't like pitchers' duels; they say they're boring. That's why the corporate riffraff over in one of the leagues invented that heretical slut of a rule, the DH—designated hitter—so people with short attention spans could actually think they were watching baseball. But, back to pitching. The best pitchers move the ball around. It is not the velocity with which they throw the ball that is so vital to gettng batters out, but the location—where the ball ends up—and the movement of the ball after it leaves the pitcher's hand and before it enters the smooth, hogan snugness of the catcher's mitt *(Sid glares at her again, she continues politely)*, unless, of course, the batter smacks it on its way.

If one pitch is thrown up and in—*(Pauses and looks around audience)*—that's high and inside—*(Pauses and looks around audience)*—that's above the strike zone and an inch from the batter's puss—*(Pauses and looks around audience)*—chin music, ya know? When the pitcher wants to back the batter off the plate? Well, another time, perhaps; that's really a question of psychophysical intimidation and pitcher-batter relationships, and I'm getting paid to cover only so much ground. Anyway, good pitching goes like this: if pitch number one is high and tight—up and in—*(Points to under Sid's chin)* remember? I just told you—then the next pitch more than likely will be down and away—*(Points, pauses, and looks around audience)*—low and outside? *(Leans out downstage and looks around)* Are you getting any of this? *(Pause)*

Look, if you're looking for a ball in a certain place, like out over the plate big and juicy *(Points to the center of Jed's mitt)*, and instead, a ball comes speeding past your nose *(Points at Sid's nose)*, up and in, more than likely you'll back off the plate a tad, and more than likely if the next one is thrown down and away, it'll look—by contrast—to be out of the strike zone, and while you might *think* it was far enough away to be called a ball, if the pitcher's any good—got any credibility—it'll be called a strike. If you swing at it, more than likely you'll swing over it. So, either way, you lose. If you're the batter. *(Nods apologetically at Sid, who glares at her)*

Anyway, next time you have a chance, look for this *(Points with pointer):* up and in, down and away. You won't be sorry. Oh, yes, and remember, just about any focus is better than none.

(Formally) Good-bye.

She poses, elbows out, as Jed and Sid each take an arm, and exits with them.

All-American

GAIL KRIEGEL

Billy Wood is dressed in a flashy sport jacket, coordinated slacks, a contrasting handkerchief in his jacket pocket, and matching socks. But everything's a bit wrinkled; there's a stain on his tie and his shirt collar is biting him in the neck. He carries a plastic bag from Seven-Eleven, a six-pack of beer in it, and a small, portable radio.

BILLY: Mr. Drucker? Billy Wood. *(Extends his hand)* Hey, thanks for giving me your time. I got to apologize for my appearance. I don't usually look so damn scuzzy but I drove right through from 'Frisco to get here this morning. Got off the freeway just now and drove right here. Oh, no, I've got a couple of accounts in Bakersville, so even if you do me the honor of just listening to what I have to say, it won't be a wasted trip. Ah, it's great to be here. I grew up in Bakersville. That is, we moved here when I was a kid. Juniper Street. The high school's right up there, right? The grade school, that way. They had a terrific baseball field. The stadium's up on Fifth. I played there a couple of times. I even remember the trophy store. I had to go pick up my high school all-American trophy myself because Coach was bummed out at me. Yeah, Bakersville. A lot of good weather here. My friend Ramond used to live right down that block where all the Mexicans live. I can see the block from here. I bet he never left this place. *(Holds up portable)* I didn't want to miss the game, but I see you got it on the TV up there. Right off the bat, we got something in common, Mr. Drucker. I brought us some beer. Oh well, you mind if I have one? Thanks. *(Opens beer, walks around store)* You've got a beautiful store here. I've never seen such good-looking merchandise. Your newspaper ad doesn't do it justice. I was thinking about your ad on the drive here. That's how I got this damn stain on my tie. I was so concentrated, I spilled my coffee and then I didn't want to meet you off the bat without a tie. . . . *(Takes tie off)* You know what's most troubling about your ad in the paper, sir? If I may . . . "Drucker's Dry Goods, a family business for sixty-five years." It's the sixty-five years that doesn't work. Sixty-five years means old and these days, people don't like old. They're afraid of looking old, they're afraid of getting old. They don't care about reliability, dependability. They'd rather shop at a fly-by-night who's going to pack up and run as long as he says NEW in his ad. Let me teach you a little lesson about consumers, Mr. Drucker. Consumers are not like fans. Fans are loyal, they're true; consumers are fickle, they're faithless. They got three religions: they got "cheap," they got "big selection," and they got "new." And "new" is especially important here in Bakersville where you got so many wetbacks. Wetbacks want "new" 'cause it makes them feel American. It's the reason they come here. They want to be like us Americans and have new clothes, new TVs, new sheets. . . . *(Looks up at the TV on the wall)* Hey, we should've made this appointment tomorrow, Mr. Drucker, after the Giants have won the pennant. *(Laughs)* They're gonna win. Oh, look at that, did you see? He's amazing, Holiday. He led the league in batting at .356, was first in on-base percentage and second in slugging. Plus, he hit .378 at home, .335 on the road, an amazing .367 with men on base and he had a .477 on-base percentage leading off innings. Amazing. Sorry. I didn't mean to carry on like that. My ex-wife said there were three of us in our marriage. Her, me, and baseball. That's why she divorced me. I used to take off on weekends. I'd fly to Michigan to see the Tigers, or Cleveland, wherever the game was hot, have a beer or two. Once it's in your blood it's like an addiction. It probably should be treated. *(Laughs. Crushes beer can and tosses it. Opens another)* These towels are like velvet, Mr. Drucker.

They don't have stuff like this up at the mall, no sir. And these linens. Hell, they feel the way sheets should feel. You know what the first thing my mother did when we moved out here? She hung the sheets out in the sun. You couldn't do that back in Chicago. These sheets feel the way my mother's did. They've got body, but they're soft. They even smell clean. Mr. Drucker, you should be too busy waiting on customers to watch this game and when you have your ad on TV you will be too busy 'cause you got some very fine merchandise here. *(Laughs)* Oh my God, look at that! Did you see that?! Even Ramond could've gotten to first base on that pitch. Ramond was the kid I was telling you about. Lived right down there. I was the only white guy on the team. All Cholos but me. They didn't like me. I was an outsider. Ramond was the only one who would be my friend. That's how those people are. Small-minded. They respected my talent, though. Mr. Drucker, I don't mean to sound like I'm bragging but I was good. Maybe I was even great. I'm not bragging. I was born with the game inside me, that's what my father used to say. That's why we moved here. The old man saw I was a natural. You give them the best opportunity. My father was no fool. He got a transfer from the post office. You ever read about Bobby Higgins? His family did the same thing. They're gonna nominate him for the Hall of Fame. I practiced every free moment I had and when there was no more daylight, my father would drive me to the K-Mart parking lot down on First. They had lights there. I was so good, when I was eleven, they traded me for a fourteen-year-old. No Little League player ever got traded. *(Opens another beer)* I love baseball. You know the best thing about playing the game, Mr. Drucker? You never know your limits. At any one time, you don't know how good you are or how good you can be. So you keep on pushing and you keep on surprising yourself. You always feel like the best is yet to come. You never achieve in life the way you do on a baseball field on a good day. Once, Mr. Drucker, we had to play the Grant League, the

Bloods from downtown. Coach says to us, "Don't be intimidated by those Niggers," but even he was intimidated. They
came out strutting. You know how those blacks are. They had
cool names and wore bandanas instead of caps on their heads.
Everyone was striking out. I got up there, Mr. Drucker, and
stared down the pitcher, then put that ball three hundred
yards over the fence. Even the Niggers cheered me. That
changed the whole game. We won, six–four, and three of
those runs were mine. If you know baseball, Mr. Drucker,
you'll know I'm not just bragging when I tell you that in one
game, I went six for six and knocked in twelve runs. Coach
had to nominate me for all-American even though he didn't
want to. He didn't like me or something. Guy was Filipino.
He had weird ideas. Ramond was good, but Cholos don't
know the game like we do. They're not as smart, they don't
have it in their blood the way we do. I did have something of
a temper, though. Once, when we were playing the team that
had all the rich kids, I got mad at the pitcher. He struck me
out in three pitches. I threw a rock at him. It was only a joke.
(Laughs) He was a Jew or maybe a Eyetalian, one of those
minorities. I didn't think it would put him in the hospital.
Nothing bad happened. It turned out he was all right. Just a
lot of blood because it hit him in the forehead. *(Opens another can of beer)* And there was a time when this kid José
Alvarez, who never got a hit off anyone, got a home run off
me. I heard the ball go thwak! against the chain-link fence
and something went thwak! in my head. I got mad and flung
a bat into the stands. It hit an old lady. Both times Ramond
said he did it. He knew the team would be all right if he had
to sit out games instead of me. *(Laughs)* Hey, you'd think I
drove all the way from S-F to tell you baseball stories.
(Cheers) Did you see that? Did you see that? This is crazy. I'm
supposed to be pitching you *(Laughs)*, not watching this
game. Well, that goes to show you the power of TV, Mr.
Drucker. It grabs your attention. It's like being up at bat. The
same way nothing comes between you and the ball, when you

watch TV, nothing comes between you and the screen. It's the most powerful media there is. Nothing else has credibility, Mr. Drucker. The world's gone crazy. Things changing every day. But not TV. TV is always there in your living room; it's steady, it's reliable. Just imagine if instead of that silly beer ad that's on right now, you see Drucker's Dry Goods. You'd be reaching thousands of people. It's true. It's a statistic. TV sells! And I'm going to save you money on your ad. We're going to get rid of the middle men: the advertising agency, the art directors, actors. That's what's expensive on TV. We'll bring the camera right into the store. Hell, if you want I'll be in the commercial. I'll walk down the aisles and sing . . . I made up this jingle as I drove here. I won't even charge you a dime for it. Now, whatever you want to add, feel free to. We're in this together; it's all about teamwork, Mr. Drucker. *(Sings to the tune of "Fugue for Tin Horns" from* Guys and Dolls*)* "I got some towels right here, some fine linens there, I got plates and pots and gadgets galore. Come on, Come in, Come on into Drucker's Dry Goods Store. . . ." Like it? You like it, Mr. Drucker? . . . "Come on, Come in, for sure you'll be back for. . . . " Oh my God! I can't believe it! He dropped the ball, Drucker! Did you see that!? He dropped it! The guy is weak! He's fucking weak! *(Opens another can)* You can't be weak! Ramond was weak. Right before a championship game, he says to me, "You and me, Billy, we're going to make the pros." Of course, I start laughing. I mean, Christ, the guy hit two home runs in his whole career. And I'm more than a little pissed that he compares himself to me. You know what he does when I tell him he's not in the same league with me? He starts to cry. Next thing I know, three of the guys on the team are holding me down and the rest of them are using me like a punching bag. Ramond was a real popular guy. And those Greasers stick together, that's one thing I'll say for them. Coach didn't even stop them. My eye was swollen, one of my knees snapped, two of my fingers was crushed and I was pitching that game.

"You're going to be a pro, Boy." I could hear my father saying that to me. "Don't be weak like them, Boy." It wasn't my best game. I didn't come to life till the top of the eighth when I see they're winning seven–six. I start throwing my torpedoes and strike out three in a row. My Spic teammates get inspired and get a run. Top of the ninth, I strike them out again and in the last inning, there's a man on first and third and I hit one home. Now, all runs are not equal, you know that, Mr. Drucker. A run you get in the bottom of the ninth when the score is tied is just not the same as any other run. Jesus, I can still hear the crowd screaming, both sides of the stands, screaming. I felt like a rock star. I thought that would smooth over the bad feelings. I mean, Jesus, so I laughed at the kid and called him a couple of names. It's all in the game. But the van took off without me. I had to hitch over fifty miles to get home. They ruined my knee. Dumb fucking foreigners. Oh, I kept playing all through high school. . . . *(Opens beer)* My grandmother used to say, "I don't care for success or even happiness for you. I only hope my children can accept their fate when they grow up." Well, you know something, Mr. Drucker? Sales and sports are the same, exactly the same. Both are competitive, both require practice, discipline, and teamwork. Yes, sir, you got to fight until the death. And you can't make no excuses, the score tells all. Christ, I hate hearing my boss say, "Don't tell me any hard-luck stories, Billy, all I want to know is did you score, Boy?" *(Long pause)* Could we turn that fucking thing off now? It's getting on my nerves! *(Game is turned off)* Look, Mr. Drucker, I'll be straight with you. You've had the same fucking ad in the newspapers since when? Maybe 1965? You're falling behind. It's the nineties now and that's it in a nutshell. In the nineties people don't read newspapers, Christ, especially not here in Bakersville where there's so many ignorant fucking wetbacks and ethnics. Most of them don't even know how to read. They watch TV. They do whatever the tube tells them. TV is the way to go, Mr. Drucker! . . . Tell me, Mr. Drucker, am I getting to first base with you?

Base Hit

ANDRÉA J. ONSTAD

YOUNG GIRL: So I'm the last person picked, even after Maryann Muller with the polio brace, and so we set out to play girls' softball in the gym, 'cause it's winter and snowing outside and we have to play even if we don't want to 'cause it's P.E. and Coach Jensen, who is the same coach for high school and coaches all the sports, baseball, basketball, football, and all the teams, the A team, the B team, the C team, he only likes the big top players like the big high school boys and ignores everybody else and he's already yawning over there by the bleachers so I know he's bored silly with us sixth-grade girls and especially with the ones who can't play, like me, I mean, I'm practically invisible, like the only reason he doesn't give me an F is that I do show up and I do try, I don't hide in the locker room and the only reason I don't, see, is because I'd be the only one 'cause everybody else, almost, except for Maryann Muller with the runted leg, are big tough farm girls and they all know how to play 'cause they play with their brothers and stuff but Coach Jensen DOES like my older sister who can't play either but she says he likes her 'cause she draws all the posters for the games and she says maybe I should start drawing and maybe he'd notice and have me draw a poster for something and then give me an A but I don't want to and anyway, how can I draw in P.E. class while we're all running around and stuff? 'Cause anyway, I like to read, like it's only January and I've read all the books in the little libraries in the back of the sixth-, seventh-, and eighth-grade rooms and just today my teacher Mrs. Beaumont let me go up to the big high school library that's like this whole room with just books and so I told Mrs. Blomberg that I wanted to read something that I wanted to think about like time and stuff 'cause I'm always asking questions like, Why doesn't time go backwards? and Why does time seem to go faster when you're playing and having fun and why does it seem to go so slow at other times like in a class where you have to get up in front of everybody and do something you hate? like now, so she helped me pick out this real interesting book called *A Brief History of Time* by this scientist she said would be a good role model for me 'cause he's in a wheelchair and stuff and can't use his arms and legs or anything but he's real smart so it doesn't matter. I got it in the locker room and I guess I could just go read it but like I said, I never miss P.E. 'cause I'd be the only one and anyway my dad says I read too much, "You're gonna ruin your eyes," he says, but I can see real good when I'm reading, I just don't see that ball real good when it's coming at me and I guess I probably do need glasses 'cause I always have to sit at the front of the class so I can see the blackboard and one time Mrs. Beaumont tested all our eyes so I memorized the chart before she came to me so I really didn't see anything and she said, just like this, "Huh, I thought you were nearsighted but it looks like you're twenty-twenty after all, huh," so I guess that meant I needed glasses but I didn't want to tell my dad 'cause he'd just say, "You put your face too close to the book. If you held it further away your eyes would get better," and then he'd say like he always does, "You read too much anyway," but anyway, I don't want glasses, I like how I see and anyway I can see the words in a book and this new one's got real little print but I can see it real good. Boy, I wish I could be reading it right now instead of sitting here waiting to bat at some dumb old ball I can hardly see at all.

So like I said, we're in the gym, which is like an all purpose gym I guess, like some schools have separate gyms for things but this one's got the basketball nets and scoreboard and pullout bleachers and then it's got this big stage where we put on class plays and have graduation and stuff and where the band plays during some of the basketball halftimes like at homecoming and the curtains are big heavy red velvet things and they're drawn tight most of the time like now and you can kind of touch them with your head if you lean back far enough if you're sitting on the edge of the stage.

So now our team is up at bat, the two captains just hand-fisted the bat and Grace Ann, the six-foot-tall sixth grader, our captain and the best grade school girl athlete, anyway, her hand was on top so we get up to bat first so I'm sitting on the edge of the stage next to Bonnie Heikkinen, she lives on the hill in a big house her dad built with a swimming pool—now swimming is something else, I can beat even Grace Ann in that, but oh no, in P.E. we have to play only the boys' ball sports, that's it—so anyway, we're sitting here on the edge of the stage, swinging our legs, and I can tell Bonnie doesn't like sitting next to me 'cause I was picked last and even though she's not such a great player 'cause she's a town girl, she's not too bad 'cause she had some brothers on the A team and Coach Jensen liked them plus she's rich and popular so she's usually a first pick so I'm swinging my legs and looking over at her socks from the corner of my eye and Bonnie feels me looking and says to me in a kind of pinched voice like she'd rather not talk to me at all, "Why're your legs all pimply like that?" so I immediately turn all red and look down at my legs and yeah, they are all pimply from the cold and raw winter and probably from the fact that I only take a bath once a week 'cause my dad has to heat the water on the stove and then we all use it so my skin gets all rough and stuff so I dunno what to say so I just say, "I dunno but I sure like your socks. Where'd you get those socks?" And she says, chomping hard on her gum, "My mom gets my socks and I don't know where she gets 'em." "Oh," I say, 'cause that's all I can think of saying then 'cause I don't have a mom so I know I'll never get socks like that but I sure like them and the way she has them folded down kind of in thirds so they bunch up around her ankle all thick and warm, not exactly bobby socks, a little neater than that and not like my thin anklets that come up to my ankle bone, stretch out all floppy, and then work their way down the back of my heel so I have to keep pulling them up out of my shoe every few steps just to keep from walking on them.

So I just sit there swinging my legs, looking at everybody's legs hanging there over the side of the stage and realize almost everybody has socks like Bonnie except the really poor kids and of course me so I figure I could ask Dad to go find me some maybe at the Co-op in town but he always says, "Oh, you don't need that," whenever I want some new clothes like he's worried I'm gonna turn into some kind of clothes-crazed girl teen so I'm sitting there swinging my legs and thinking about socks and I hear Grace Ann yelling, "Batter up! Batter up!" and pretty soon I hear Coach Jensen hollering, "Batter up! Batter up!" and then I hear Grace Ann starting to sound really mad and she's growling, "Who's up next?! I said, who's up next?!!" And then Bonnie gives me a push and I see Maryann Muller, who was picked just before me so in the batting lineup she bats just before me and she's over there on first base with her brace and all and it dawns on me—it's me! I'm up next!—so I run over to get the bat, swinging it kinda tough like I know what I'm doing except what I'm really doing is chopping the air like a lumberjack chops wood and then I'm next to the plate and Grace Ann whispers to me, "Bases loaded. Two outs. You gotta do something this time even if you hafta walk." "Maryann musta walked," I say. "No," Grace Ann says, "Weren't you watching? What's the matter with you? Maryann got a hit!" and I looked over at Maryann and think, "Wow! Maryann got a hit and even ran all the way to first base! Wow!" and then I look over at second base and third base and all the last picks, the worst players in the sixth grade are all on base and it's up to me, the very worst player in sixth grade and probably in the world, it's up to me to get them in so I'm standing there facing the pitcher, a big tough girl, Diane Anderson, who's got seven older brothers and she's tall, not as tall as Grace Ann but almost, with about fifty more pounds on her, heck, she looks almost like a grown-up lady, and here I am, skinny, pimply legged, socks sagging under my heels, blind as a headless chicken, and ready to chop at that old ball so old Diane winds up and she underhands the big fat thing and lets go a slow one, so slow it practically stands still in one spot for a whole minute before it starts coming, wobbling like a big white flying saucer in slow motion, aiming right for me like it's gonna hit me right in the kisser and so right away I start chopping away at it, not once but a whole bunch of times, "Get away from me! Get away from me!" and I can hear old Coach starting to yell, "Strrrrrrrrrri—" 'cause he's not even looking 'cause he does that automatically when I'm at bat, and somehow I manage to hit that big soft thing! and it goes bouncing like a ping pong ball 'cause I hit it with my chop, almost pounding it into the ground! and I'm so stunned I even hit the thing that I stand there for a second, watching it bounce once, twice, and then right up into the fat face of Diane Anderson, hitting her right smack in the glasses and they pop and break and dangle from their black rubber athletic band, kind of bouncing there on her big bosomy chest and while she's fumbling around all blind like me now, someone is yelling, "Run! Run!" and I hear lots of voices yelling, "Run! Run!" so I start running to first and I see Maryann hobbling to second and I realize I have the bat in my hand so I start to loosen my grip on the wood and I feel it slipping, slipping, and just as I hear it hit the floor, my foot touches first base and I hear Grace Ann yell, "Don't drop the bat! Don't drop the bat!" and the bat hits the floor making a big hollow wood-on-wood sound and then it rolls with a kind of clop-clop-clop-clop-clop that's really loud 'cause by this time everybody's quiet because dropping the bat in the gym, on that sprung wood floor that cost so much we got all kinds of lectures about what shoes to wear on it and all so as not to mark it up, like dropping the bat like that, like now, when we're playing in the dead of winter, is an automatic out.

You're supposed to hand the bat to the bat catcher waiting there on the way to first base.

So I'm standing there on first base, forgetting that rule of course and thinking, "Wow, I got a hit and we got a run! Wow!" and then my team is walking past me to the field, looking right through me like I'm a ghost or something and I'm wondering what's going on and no one's talking to me and everything's so quiet and slowed down like every second is an hour and I start walking off first, real slow, like I'm underwater or something, and head for the outfield, past the basketball nets, way to the back of the gym, and when I see the door there, open just a crack, I slink through it and all of a sudden time speeds up again, even faster than normal, and I'm running as fast as I can and the sweat's pouring off me and I'm running and running and running and then all of a sudden I'm in the locker room and I stop and it's like I'd never left the locker room, like none of this happened, like time DID go backwards and so I open my locker and get out my book and start reading like I shoulda done in the first place.

Wait Till Next Year

LILLIAN MORRISON

I would like to walk away from you
like a pitcher after a 1.2.3 inning
heading for the dugout
poker-faced with power.

But it's not a grass diamond
we play on, not a fenced-off place
where umpires see to it
that fair is fair.

We struggle in the pitted, unbounded
field of emotion. No referees.
The errors we make are not put up
on a scoreboard and forgotten.

As a fielder of bad bounces, I'm only
so-so. Life isn't much like a ball game
no matter what the song says.
Still, "It ain't over till it's over."

My rookie days are long gone
But I still look forward to new innings
a few more happy recaps
to play in my mind over and over again.

The Swinging Marilyns

CYNTHIA L. COOPER

The time is the future. A woman enters, wearing a wig and dressed to look like Marilyn Monroe. She speaks to an unseen person, an interviewer.

MARILYN: You might think it's a bit holo-polo that the league started with me. Singing the league anthem. But there's a reason for everything, isn't there? *(Looks as if she's going to sing, stops)*

I must say I never lifted a bat in my life. I was married to Joe. For a short while. And he was a hero in the old leagues. And he had a bat. But the two of us didn't last long. Not because of the singing. That was the acting. See, this one time I had a little bitty acting job and flipped my skirt in the air before one of those blower machines and he gets all huffy and puffy. He says now that I'm married to him, I'm not supposed to be working; I'm supposed to be at home. That was the end of me and Joe. And I was long . . . long . . . what's the way to say this? . . . gone . . . when the song took over the leagues.

Girls! *(Calls offstage as if to musicians, sings or talk-sings lightly)*

"A kiss on the hand . . ."—I really enjoy this song—"may be quite Continental . . ."

She turns, humming if necessary, removing the wig and clothing, emerging as JONI.

Some people will tell you the ball girls began it all when they commandeered the locker rooms. But it was Marilyn. Always Marilyn.

Let me tell you straight. Marilyn's voice was not very good, but she had a way of getting a song inside your head, like whispers that took hold of you and built up a power, became gale force winds pushing you along without regard to the consequences. You might say her voice became an idea that got to us one year and wouldn't let go. Those words lived like an exclamation mark waiting to happen, like a cheer way down that you were holding, just holding, until the moment you could let it out.

(Yells offstage as if watching someone there) All right. You're leaning in too much. Keep your back straight!

(Returning to interviewer) In 1998 women were still doing things like "taking their daughters to work." But the thing is dads stopped taking their sons to ball games back in 1994. Strike on. The dads complained. Politicians and writers— big-name people—whined that they couldn't live out their dreams of playing the major leagues. Strike's over. They pouted. They still didn't go. Stands were empty, except for a few isolated places here and there—Cleveland. The thrill was gone. The nostalgia was ruptured. Where was Joe DiMaggio? But Marilyn was still waiting.

(Yells offstage) Try Debbie's bat. Good. Yeah. That one.

(To interviewer) Same time, boys stopped showing up at the summer camps. If you want to have a camp, you have to field some teams. So the camps started loading up with girls. By 1997, there weren't any players except girls. So many girls that they decided they better get women coaches. Which is where I came in. So you might say the daughters got us the work. And some of the players were incredible, really hot. We had three sisters, Bonnie and Sally and Evie Ericson. Norwegian, from Minnesota. Hit like the ball was ice waiting to be whacked off a low-hanging tree branch in the winter, instead of a flying object coming at them. Evie, the youngest, was one of the girls got hired as ball girl in St. Louis. And I can't tell you how important that was.

I think Bonnie, Sally, and Evie were all at the camp on

the stormy night we decided to play some classic movies on the VCR for relaxation. *Gentlemen Prefer Blondes* was one of the tapes someone had grabbed at Gladys's Quick Shop and Video Store, although the girls at the camp weren't quite in that mold. We were just about to pop that one out and throw in *Die Hard Two*. And some of them said, oh leave it in, and others just laughed, and said, yeah, do it. So we watched, tired from the workouts, passing popcorn, making little mental reminder notes about improvements in plays from that afternoon, and when those words came out of Marilyn, everyone gasped. Right there, we recognized, all at once, in unison, the sense of possibility.

(Repeating but not singing) "A kiss on the hand . . . may be . . ."

(Calling offstage) Come on, women. No maybes about it. The Pirates have nothing on us. We built the Cardinals from nothing. Remember that.

(Back to interviewer) All my life I wanted to be a player. I wanted like heck to play in a big stadium carrying the banner of some city; stand by second base, wearing my uniform, swaying side to side, showing I was the best shortstop. *(Enthusiastically takes a momentary stance, then shrinks back)* They called me all kinds of names for wanting that, I don't have to tell you. Anyhow, my playing time was over by 1999 when the hot dogs turned sour and the sauerkraut wilted in every stadium in the country.

(Gesturing as if, "picture this") Despair's setting in. No one's having fun—not fans or owners or players or sports writers. There is so little fun in baseball that no one looked up from their sky boxes to see that we don't have any students at the camp that summer. We have graduates. From three dozen states. College girls. Over twenty-five colleges. The best. Every island. Every nook. Every cranny. Every summer league, tucked away in every Prospect Park or Como Park or Metropark. We gathered the girls of summer. By then, we've had months to make out our takeover plan.

I was one of the people to address them, the first night. *(As if doing so)* Our financial backers are trying, but they can't get any movement in the market. We have to do something dramatic to get action. Some of the coaches started talking. We wanted a friendly takeover, one that wows everyone with its panache, builds fans. We made out a game plan.

(As if pointing to a board) So I now unveil to you: the Marilyn plan.

(Addressing interviewer) Immediate success. Well, there's one hitch. Not everyone agrees to dye their hair blonde. I suppose this is the biggest internal dispute. Originally we thought uniformity would show our universal agreement, make a statement. But ours is a multicultural group, and let's face it, Marilyn's was not. Some of the players would have felt pretty awful. So we have the idea for the wigs. We made blonde-styled Marilyn wigs, red Marilyn wigs, black Marilyn wigs, and even a couple of hair weaves.

Next we set ourselves up as the before-game entertainment. Before-game entertainment was something that the owners were trying because they were so desperate to get people to the games. And we offer ourselves without a fee— FREE entertainment. Well, you can imagine how the baseball owners fell for this. We decide to pick someplace where we can count on the ball girls and will have the least fan resistance. St. Louis seems like a natural. So we bill ourselves as the "Swinging Marilyns" and make up a little brochure with all of us in top hats, fake bat-shaped canes, and baseball uniforms—you know, like we were "make-believing." And at the summer camp, we choreograph a few high kicks here and there—not with the catchers, mind you, because they didn't have the legs for that kind of thing.

And we aim for just before the All-Star Game when the season is seeming pretty long and boring no matter how good it is. What can I tell you? It all worked perfectly.

(As if it is that day) Fans are gathering in the stands. We take our places on the field as the before-game entertainment.

All in a long line. Someone announces us. "And now for your entertainment, the Swinging Marilyns." We do a single kick to the left, then to the right, begin to sing our song. The second refrain is the cue for the ball girls. Evie Ericson is the point person for the ball girls. No one's watching them, 'cause pretty much all eyes are fixed on us. The ball girls do their part brilliantly, pulling out battery-powered drills and putting locks on the field side of the locker room doors in under fifty seconds to keep any of the other players from coming out. Perfect. Evie signals us that they're done. And then the "Swinging Marilyns" toss off their hats and one by one, we run out to the bleachers. Our people there give us whatever we need—caps, mitts, gum—and then each girl takes her place on the field or in the dugout or in the pitching pen or sidelines, like me. The music is still playing and we all run quite jovially, as if this is part of the performance. We're at first, at second, in the outfield—we're at home. And then when everyone is in place, we all yell loud, over and over: "DIAMONDS ARE A GIRL'S BEST FRIEND. DIAMONDS ARE A GIRL'S BEST FRIEND."

At the bases and all, we cheer on the crowd, waving, and get the people in the stands to join in. And they do. "DIAMONDS ARE A GIRL'S BEST FRIEND." (Then, singing, Marilyn-style) "Diamonds are a girl's best friend." Our people in the booth take the microphone in hand, and slipping past the national anthem, yell, "Ladies. . . . Play Ball." Everyone in the stands is so worked up at this point, that they just cheer.

(As if leaving that day, addressing the interviewer) After that, pretty much the rest of the leagues fell one-two-three. Like a no-hitter. Our financial people swept through, made offers, bought stock, did whatever.

And that's the way it went. So, if you want my opinion on it, I think Marilyn would forgive us. She was a working girl, too; the best. In fact, I think she'd stand up in the middle of the stadium, like everyone else does these days in the

American League and the National League when they hear that song and the players run out of the locker room and take their places. . . .

Turning as in the beginning, putting on wig, revolving around as Marilyn, speaking in a Marilyn voice.

Hey there, you girl, come on and SLUG it, come on and slug one for me! *(Jumps, as if cheering, music rises)*

A Conversation in Center Field

JEFFERY SCOTT ELWELL

The play opens in darkness. A voice can be heard singing a jazzed-up version of "The Star-Spangled Banner": Ohoh, say can you seeeeee! by the dawn's early liiiggghhhhtttt! What so proudly we hailed . . . at the twi-light's last gleaming. Whose broad stripes and bright stars. . . . The voice ceases abruptly as the lights zoom up on a center fielder, looking up and pounding his glove enthusiastically.

CENTER FIELDER: Come on, baby. Come to Papa! *(Flipping up his sunglasses and addressing the audience)* It looks easy, don't it? Come on. Admit it. You think this is child's play. You think a punk like me that barely made it through high school shouldn't be making a million two and driving a gold-plated Mercedes. Go ahead, you ain't gonna hurt my feelings none. That's right. I'll just laugh about it all the way to the bank. You. Yeah, you, fat white boy. You keep sittin' in your field box, eatin' hot dogs and drinkin' Budweisers and tellin' all your friends how great an athlete you were in college, how you'd be out here if it weren't for that bum knee. Shit! The only thing you'd be doin' on this field is chalkin' the lines. *(Laughing but suddenly getting serious)*

God made me for this. *(Flipping down his sunglasses and racing back to make a catch)* See . . . *(He throws the ball back in)*

What'd I tell you? God gave me speed so I can race down a fly ball like a cheetah drawin' a bead on a hot lunch. He gave me eyes like an eagle so I can pick up that tiny white ball in mid-flight. He gave me an arm like a rifle to gun down some lead-assed catcher tryin' to take home on a shallow fly. He gave me all that and what'd He give you? A fat ass to sit on? A big mouth to curse me with? I am one of God's creatures. One of His great creations and what you do? Boo me? Do you boo a cheetah when he comes up empty? You boo an eagle when he drops a field mouse? Hell, no! *(Pauses)* Think about it. How'd you like to do your job in front of forty-five thousand people? Watchin' every move you make . . . razzin' you half the time . . . cussin' you out. . . . *(Addressing someone in the audience)* What about you, lady? How'd you like it if me and forty-five thousand of my friends dropped in while you was typing up a report? Just sittin' around eatin' hot dogs and drinkin' beer and booing every time you made a mistake? Cussin' out your mama. Callin' out things that'd make you red in the face. Dumpin' beer on you. You get the idea? *(Picking out another audience member)* Or what about if me and the boys stopped by the house when you was makin' dinner? Questioning your choice of seasoning? Commenting on your place settings? You think you'd enjoy that? No? Me neither. And that ain't even the worst of it. It's them vultures up there. . . . *(Points up to the press box)* Them wannabes. Most of them couldn't play nothing more athletic than chess in school and now they's the experts. They write about how you're in a slump because you didn't work out enough in the offseason. Or how you've never reached your potential.

At least you had a potential . . . you've played in the big leagues . . . you've heard the cheers. Who in the hell's gonna cheer some overweight guy with mustard stains on his polyester shirt? I mean, at least you fans, you gotta pay real money to come out to the ballpark. You got the right to be upset when we blow a game. But them writers. They get paid to eat hot dogs and drink beer and ask us stupid questions. You ever listen to some of the questions they ask? *(Becoming the writer)*

"How'd you feel when you struck out to end the game with the winning run on third base?"

(As himself) How the hell do you think I feel? Lousy, that's how. Nobody likes to lose. Nobody likes to strike out or make an error or get picked off base. It happens, though. We're human . . . we make mistakes . . . and what do we get? Booed off the field. Cussed out. Asked stupid questions by dumbass writers. That's why I don't talk to 'em. Nope, not since last season. Just got tired of it one day and stopped. Cold turkey. *(Laughing)* Now they say I'm moody. Sullen. A loner. They talk about demons I'm battling. Hell, they're the closest thing to demons that I got to deal with. I figure they're gonna write what they're gonna write about so why should I play along with their game?

Wilma "Willie" Briggs

SUSAN E. JOHNSON
From *When Women Played Baseball*

"WILLIE" BRIGGS: Max came to coach Fort Wayne in 1950 and 1951. He was a great base stealer, so he had everyone running. I stole twenty-nine or thirty bases in 1950, and I don't think I stole two the year before.

I played for him for two years. He taught me to bunt and how to fake a bunt. "Don't give it away," he'd say. When you bunt as a sacrifice, just to move the runner along, you turn around and give yourself help connecting with the ball. But when you're bunting for a base hit, you don't want anybody in the ballpark to know you're gonna bunt. So you stand up there like you're really gonna go for it. Of course, you've got to deaden the ball so it doesn't roll a mile. I'd be four steps out of there, and my bat is just hitting the ball!

I loved bunting behind Eisen. If I was out, it was a sacrifice. If I was safe, it was a hit. I couldn't lose.

I don't know how he had the patience. He spent hours and hours with me. In batting practice, everybody else would hit five, bunt two. I'd bunt five and hit two until I learned to do it. So you can see why I liked Max Carey.

When I went home I taught my brothers how to do it. My left-handed brother Jerry was a good little ball player, and became the best bunter in his softball league. He'd say, "My sister taught me!"

Since I was left-handed, Max taught me to block the catcher out. With a runner on first, a left-handed batter could get in the way just enough so that catcher didn't know when the runner was stealing. You go after the ball, and then you just kind of turn and back up. The catcher has to step a little bit to the side to see around you. But you have to do it on every single pitch; it has to become part of your natural move. Otherwise the umpire's gonna say you're obstructing. If it's part of your natural movement, and the catcher hits you, that's her problem; you're not obstructing. Little things like that give you the edge.

Max kinda had a system with us. If Tiby's on first, my job batting behind her is to get her on second. She was supposed to steal, because Max didn't want me wasting a hit to move her to second.

I could also protect her if she didn't steal. I could place the ball pretty well and keep her from being forced out. He wasn't depending on my power; he was depending on me to move her over to the next base, one way or another, for the power behind me to bring her in.

So Tiby and I had our own signal. She'd just go down her skirt and touch the hem, and that meant this is her pitch, she's gonna go on this one. So I don't swing. When she'd get to second by stealing, now I could either drop a bunt or gloss a bunt. When I bunt, I'm bunting to beat it out, not for a sacrifice. Suppose I look like I'm gonna bunt, but I hold the bat back and they call it a ball. Now the third baseman's coming in, sometimes Tiby could steal behind the third baseman.

So now Max says, "Maybe if the third baseman's playing back, drop the bunt. If she's playing in on the end of your bat, gloss the bunt." So we had another thing, just look at the third baseman and let her position tell us what to do next.

Now here's this runner that was on first is now on third. 'Course I probably got two strikes on me by now. But I've moved her two bases. And although she's done the runnin', I did my job, too. I helped her by what I did and didn't do at the plate. It didn't matter if I then grounded out, or popped out, or struck out on the next pitch. I got two batters behind me that can bring her in. To do what you were supposed to do. You cannot imagine how exciting that was to me!

I made a lot of sacrifices by batting second. My job wasn't to get hits. A good hitter is very selective, she waits for a pitch she really likes. Well, I couldn't do that. My pitch was always gone before I had a chance to swing! But if we win, who cares?

So then Max said, "You need to learn to hit down the third-base line," which I could never do being a left-handed batter. Well, he taught me that. Now, I'm left-handed, right? And I had a very closed stance. *(Willie has jumped to her feet now and has assumed her batting stance. Her hands are together on the imaginary bat, holding it high, cocking it a little, keeping loose for the incoming pitch)* Now most of the time, I'd come around like this and really pull the ball. *(She swings from her heels, hitting the imaginary ball just a little ahead of the plate)* Max said, "Stand the same way, but now you're gonna hit the ball after it's come back even with you, almost by you." He taught me how to do that. And that was really exciting. Third basemen like Al Pollitt and Jackie Kelley would be out there, off balance, rockin' back and forth. "We never knew if you were gonna bunt or not. If we moved in, you hit by us. We never knew what to do with you."

Jimmy Foxx had me batting fourth, he had me third, he had me fifth, and I wasn't doing anything. Finally one night he asked us, and we said, "If Tiby and I got first and second. . . ." We went out that night like old times. It was so refreshing!

I played with Tiby, both sides of her, right field and sometimes left field to her center field. We never had a collision. Max taught us. If the ball is hit in the air between you, so that neither one can call it, you just decided ahead of time what you're gonna do. Otherwise you're gonna kill each other out there. We decided she would get it. I would back up. So if we didn't hear a call it was automatic: it's yours, Tiby. Dive after it, do what you want to because you know I'm gonna be behind you.

If the ball went between us on the ground, are we both gonna run and both try to pick it up? No, one of us is gonna stop. We know which one's gonna get there first by where it's hit, so the other one stops, turns around, finds the play, and then tells her where she's gonna throw it before she ever picks it up.

The thought had never occurred to me that from right field you could throw a runner out at first base. Well, suppose you have a right-handed hitter up, so you're playing a little shallower than you would for a leftie. Dottie Schroeder, our shortstop, says to me, "When you get a line drive on one hop, and you're charging after it, just keep going. Throw the ball to first an throw 'em out." She said, "You know, Rose Gacioch does that."

So every time a line drive would come at me Dottie would scream, "Throw 'em out at first, Gacioch!" The first time she scared me. She wanted to make sure I was alive, awake to do it.

The most devastating time, Schroeder screams, I come charging in, boy I go after that ball . . . and I missed it. It just kept right on goin'. I bet whoever that batter was ended up with a triple. Well, Dottie and I roomed together, so when we got home she says, "Didn't throw her out, did you, Rosie?"

Dottie tells everybody about my worst play, the worst play I was ever in. I was the runner on third base, Betty Foss was on second, there's one out or nobody out. The batter just hit a little routine ground ball back to the pitcher. The pitcher picks it up, looks at me—I'm not gonna go anywhere— and Betty comes charging around third base and passed right by me. This thing goes by me like . . . I'm glad she didn't hit me, they'd still be picking up the pieces. She was out from here to the wall.

Oh, that was funny. I mean, it was funny, but it wasn't funny.

My father would try to come out once every year. This happened the first time he ever saw me play professional baseball. I knew somebody from the family was there because I'd seen the car, but I couldn't spot them in the stands. Then the game began and I forgot about it. During the game I made a shoestring catch. I was lucky, but nonetheless, it was a good catch! So when the game is over my father doesn't say, "Hello" or "That was a great catch!" he says, "Lucky catch."

The last time he ever saw me play I hit a grand-slam home run in South Bend. It not only went over the fence and out of the ballpark but over the parked cars behind the fence. I knew where he was sitting at that game, behind third base, and my mother was there too. When I circled the bases and was coming from second to third I was looking right at him. He takes off his hat, throws it down on the ground and shakes his head like, "I can't believe this." When the game is over he doesn't say, "Nice hit," he says to me, "Lucky hit!" It was really exciting for them, so I was glad.

I don't think there'll ever be another women's baseball league because they won't be able to enforce any rules and regulations. I just don't think they'd be able to find enough women that will say, "We'll do just what you want us to do in the public's eye."

Now I'm not saying that today we would make the players play in skirts. They'd be out of place today. But there are other things, like not drinking too much, you don't smoke in public, you dress for the occasion.

I think the point of those rules was to make sure the public saw us as girls and not men. They wanted us to be a class act. They wanted us to be women but play like men.

Madagascar Butterfly

ELEANORE C. SPEERT

Janice is in her fifties, telling her daughter about life when Janice was younger.

JANICE: It was a glorious day! The sky was blue, the grass was green. We watched the stadium get bigger and bigger as we walked the half mile from the parking lot to the ramp inside. Big letters over the entrance way, big walkways, big popcorn, big sodas, big people, a million seats. . . . We were in the bleachers, way up there. Brooks was on third, Weaver was pacing the dugout, all was right with the world.

You couldn't tell who they were, really, not from our seats. Well, except for Boog, because he was large and had that name. And the sounds, uh, I mean, it's just like they tell you. The crack of the bat, the rolling roar of the crowd. That roar is so fascinating to a kid. You look away from the plate and study the heads out in left field, trying to figure out the exact point of origin. You even try to watch the sound waves bounce! Try a little harder and you've missed Etchebarren running the bases and crossing the plate, or Palmer intercepting a bunt! Baseball was to watch passion without contact; no roughhousing, no pain. It was graceful, easy to understand, cheap, and outside. The stakes weren't high— well, not to me, what did I know. I never liked high stakes, it's a false god.

So you'd go to the stadium and MARVEL at the men there with transistors plastered to their ears. Why bring a radio? You're at the stadium! It's so you can hear the announcers call the game. Well, that was ridiculous! You could see the whole thing in front of you!

And sometimes, out of those same transistors, you'd hear the music. The Motown voices that made you saunter across the bedroom floor, that made you believe in romance, that made you want to learn line dances. You know, music can define your childhood. You can memorize lyrics at a young age and I can sing them for you now and not miss a beat. The Supremes, Temps, Miracles, Pips, The Vandellas. We were young, middle-class girls, walking home after school in our shirtwaist dresses and Nancy Drew hairdos, singing the harmony from the latest Four Tops hit. *(Slower)* It's what those days were. Well, sometimes. Baseball and music. Everybody tried hard. Everyone around me seemed to get some of what they wanted.

(She perks up again) Most times we'd go to the games by radio. Aretha Franklin after school, then at bedtime, under the covers for the night games. That's when my sister and I revealed to each other that we were both in love with Paul Blair. We imagined him handsome, dashing, shy, athletic— well, he'd have to be. . . . Riding home from somewhere, Sheila and I sitting in the way back seat of our tan Chevrolet wagon, we begged Mother to turn on the game. And there, right then, Paul Blair was up at bat. Our lttle hearts were racing. He hits a double, runs the bases, the crowd goes wild. So do we, bouncing up and down. Listening to the announcer sing his praises, we discovered something neither of us knew, I don't know why: "Paul Blair's a Negro!!??" we both shouted. "What'dya think?" Mother said. "But we're both in *love* with Paul Blair!" not realizing what I was saying. "Well, one of you better give him up," she said. "You know," Sheila came back, "we'd know these things if you'd let us watch TV!"

I knew all the words to the Supremes' songs, and with our new TV privileges I was soon working on the players' numbers. Sheila and I got the small TV in our room, and, going to bed earlier than most kids, we would pretend to talk before sleep as we usually did, but really watch the games with the sound off. Then, one night, one WORLD

SERIES night—can you believe we had to go to bed at our regular time on a World Series night?—we hear: "Do you girls have that TV on in there?" Mom yelled up. We looked at each other; I yelled back, "No." . . . That was it. I lied! Nothing happened. *(This triggers something; sadly)* Things happened later.

(Perking up again) And the soundtrack was always playing. James Brown, Sam and Dave, Little Stevie, Dobie Grey.

Later it was Eddie Murray. What a guy. What a smile; you could melt butter with that smile. He should have used it more, rattle the competition. Nobody smiles when they play anymore. Then it was Ripkin. It wasn't hard to spot him when he was young. That picture I have of him? The one I took on the last game at the old stadium? It got everybody talking. Hung it right by the door. Anybody who walked in the house, saw that photo, started talking baseball.

You know what it was? Baseball had integrity; one of the lost arts of civilization. I didn't have to know those guys off the field and I didn't want to! And the music? . . . the same civility, no matter how bad your heart ached. . . .

Before Dallas, in the early sixties, people talked of heroes all the time. Elvis, Hitchcock, the Kennedy clan, Picasso, even that family that walked the high wire. Kids would look up to Einstein, Shepard, to Salk, Updike, the Beatles, but me . . . someone would ask me who I thought was a hero? I'd tell 'em: "The Robinson brothers: Frank, Brooks, and Smokey."

(She is tired. Slowly she sits down) What was it about the game, about the music? Character, class, easy love—the kind you fell into and when you made a mistake someone forgave you and you lived happily ever after. Oh, sure, occasionally someone got killed on a motorcycle, but that made us appreciate what we had all the more.

One game at a time, one song at a time, one step at a time. The way to build a life. . . . *(Getting agitated)* Why do I remember this? I need to remember the time of day, that a palm is not an oak, that milk goes in the refrigerator, that I am a woman, not a fish. I need to concentrate. . . . One day at a time, Janice, one hour at a time, one minute. *(She looks up and sees Rachel)* You took your first steps at two. How old was I? Can you remember back that far? I remember you. I remember Sheila. She's gone now. I can *only* remember her; I can't bring her back. . . . *(Pause)* So why do I remember you? Why?

Custer

ROBERT INGHAM

FREDERICK WILLIAM BENTEEN: More than anything else on this old planet, I do dearly love the game of baseball. I'd go anywhere to watch anybody play baseball. We had the best baseball team on the High Plains: my troop, H Troop, Seventh Cavalry. Played baseball in some of the damndest places. Once, in the summer of '75, we were sent into the Black Hills to break up this party of miners who'd settled unlawfully, confiscate their equipment, and escort them out. And as we were standing around, going through the formalities, one of these mining fellows notices a piece of baseball equipment attached to the saddle of one of my fellows. And, as you might expect, the subject of wagers soon arose, and, as you might expect, it was soon proposed that we play them for the confiscated equipment. Well, I couldn't see my way clear to that, it now being government property and I the custodian only; but I said that if they wanted to raise a pot from private pocket, we would endeavor to match same. And so they did, and so did we, and we played them, out there in the middle of nowhere. And wouldn't you know, God being the sort of fellow that he is, we skunked those poor boys? I mean, humiliated them? Three hundred and thirty-seven thousand to nothing! It was embarrassing. And so, they rode away, turned back from a fortune in gold, confiscated of several thousands of dollars in equipment, and taken for every cent they had in private pocket as well. I sometimes think if we'd had any charity in us at all, we'd have thrown the game. Let those poor boys have something. But if it had been proposed to me at the time, I would have beaten the proposer to death with the catcher's mask. Fierce ball players!

Missing

GAY DAVIDSON-ZIELSKE

A frowsy woman of about seventy sits on a bleacher facing the audience. The shadow of a backstop falls over her throughout the scene. Occasionally, a boyish voice razzes somebody—"He can't hit. He can't hit. What a girl. Swing, batter, batter, batter," etc. A low voice comes up quaveringly.

WOMAN: Hey! Yeah, son, you. Oh, don't worry. I'm old enough to be your grandmother. Might *be* your grandmother. There, that's a good boy. You know, that guy *(Gestures)* deserved to strike out. He swings like a rusty gate. *(Beat)* I know you won't believe this, but there was a time I never struck out once. Was a time this fanny never fanned, never warmed a bench for longer than . . . nine. *(Laughs, but bitterly)* Then I turned "pro." Yep, I was the one who put the "Pro" in "Pro-hib-i-shun." And I never walked! Body never walked. Nope. If I went anyplace, I ran. Actually, I was on the run most of my life. Done a little stint down . . . Georgia. Good state, Georgia. Home of the Georgia Peaches. Actually was on the road with the Peaches when I got into trouble. No wait, I know you don't want to hear about my problems. Stick around. What? Pictures? Sure *(Pulls out dog-eared mugshots).* Look! I got pictures. You bet. Front and side. Side's my choice. Shows my curls. Curl and hurl, that's me. I could pitch it like nobody's business. Hey! *(Tosses mugshots on the ground, but pauses to check unseen boy's face against another piece of paper)* Wasn't just A. Nor triple-A. Was in A.A. Bunch of Bible-beatin', bleatin' crackers. Have to pray to get a neck of chicken so stringy you could choke. No, actually, that was the Salvation Army I meant right then. Wusn't A.A. after all.

Same difference. Hey, you got a good swing there. Choke up, though. You don't wanta dip like that. *(Sound of boy, razzing)*

That's the stuff. Hold it lighter. You ain't got to choke that chicken, boy. You don't know what it's like to watch the younger, smarter ones score, though, in the end. They said I was a ringer. Hum dinger. Hummer. Dinger. You know. *(Beat)* You don't? Say, what's in the bag? Got them Golden Archers on the side. Boy, I knew bags. Made the round of bags. Touched the bags, ever one. Now, I turned into a bag, lad. Hey, "bag lad, bag dad." Not bad for Good Friday. *(She laughs, too loudly)*

Sound of a solid hit, cheering. She jumps up, strewing posters she's been holding. There are two pictures, one showing a woman of about forty-five who resembles the woman on the bench and the other showing a boy who has been "computer-morphed" to look about age seventeen, with a headline, "Missing."

Hey, you must be sixteen at least. What? I saw you drive up. If you got a permit, you would be at least sixteen. Do you know any boys who look like this? *(Holds up picture. A beat)* Well, that's because it's one of them computer things—not my real grandson. How about the woman? Might be one of your friends' mom? Oh come on. I'm not gonna harm you. Whoops! There you go! You're up! Hey, knock a homer for an old lady. Knock one for your mom. A triple at least. *(Mutters)* Wish I'd never gotten to third base. I shoulda gone home. Should always go home. *(Beat)* Please, come home.

A Changing Season

JAMES R. MILLER

MAN: I never gave a damn about the game—the mindless masses
huddled cold and damp on splintered wooden seats in rainy
weather, the red slap of the sun on your back on endless summer afternoons. One inning, three outs, and it all made
sense. Dollars and cents. As far back as I can remember, it
was always the money that mattered to me.

You see, when you're a gambling man it's all about who
covers the number spread, it doesn't matter who wins or loses
or how fair they play. Not even with the home team. Not
even with your own life.

Last Thursday, a letter came addressed to my bar, from a
suburb of Chicago that hadn't existed when I grew up, and an
area I've never been to. It was from a woman who called herself my daughter, and it was an invitation back to a life that I
had long ago lost to chance.

Your grandson loves baseball, the woman wrote, and she
remembered from her own mother's stories that so did I.
Maybe, she thought, I could take him to a Cubs game. It
would be a start, she said. No promises, she said. Just call.

And so I did.

But what that boy knew to be baseball and the game I
played merely shared the same name.

The truth be known, I had never even been to a stadium.

When I was a boy I never saw the blue of the sky melt
into the deep gray of the steel stands, and I only imagined the
steam off the vendors' red-hots. During the post-Depression
era it was security that mattered, and that meant money, as
much as you could get your hands on. And the riskiest, the
most daring thing imaginable, would be to gamble on the

chance for more, with no thought to the possibility of watching it all slip away. Now that was a game. Baseball just happened to provide a nice backdrop.

As I grew older, the open air of a stadium seemed from another world, and the only colors that existed behind my office door were the black of the lead of my pencil and the white of the rice paper as it disappeared in a water-pail grave. And then there were dollar bills, the color of green, coming and going like the ebb and tide of an endlessly retreating sea.

People would play the bases betting a dime, two dimes, some for thousands each time. I never became the best bookie in town, but I was dependable, and I owned a bar on the west side of the big city. Some folks, they would travel as far as the south side to visit—lots of people coming in on weekends to place their bets. I would run the odds up, going fifty-thousand on each side, getting my commission on each, you see. When it came to the money, I was always sure to win. But for the bettors, the odds were never in their favor. Only a few returned Wednesdays to collect their share of winnings, and rarely were they the same smiling faces.

But they don't keep building Vegas because people win.

Nobody wins.

White, black, and green. They were all the colors I needed to see rainbows where there were storms, happy faces where there lay masked misery.

But who can predict the future? Nobody. Not in baseball, and definitely not in life.

The problem with baseball is it's the one game you can lose the most. Not even horse racing or football can come close to a bat and ball. I've seen lives crushed in a single, sunny Monday afternoon. Take the Cubs and the Mets. The money line on a good day was a two-hundred-dollar bet just to win back another hundred. If the Cubs didn't cover the spread it would take a man two more wins just to make his loss back. What's the odds on that? And most couldn't afford to lose—it was the rent money, the kid's grocery bill, or a social security check.

Money wasn't my deficit, I always got ten percent. My losses were more gradual than that, not days but years turning to decades of wasted time, not money—but flesh and blood, even life itself. In the end, the damage I surveyed was more complete than the sorriest weekend loser I had ever seen. All the things I thought would surround my life later had somehow been edged into another bet and been gambled away.

I was thirty-five years old when my wife and child left, and any hope I had for happiness disappeared with them.

Things faded softly to gray as the world grew newer and this physical prison became wrinkled and aged. My hair began to soften to silver in every mirror I checked, tinting it whiter and whiter with the years. There were no strangers stopping by the bar any longer, rice paper was replaced by laptop computing, cell phones. Cops weren't beating down doors, they just didn't care anymore. And frankly, dammit, neither did I.

But I still played on.

And at seventy-one years old I took one more gamble and found myself alone with a child I had never seen, and in a place I had long ago stopped imagining.

Inside the stadium it was all there, the green grass fields with powder white lines, runners were stealing bases, batters were changing hands for wooden sticks, the smell of the open air, fans cheering, cheering for the chance to make it big, to score, to be rich, or maybe, this time, just to be happy.

I watched that game, not through eyes weathered by time and statistics, but through the fresh young eyes of the child. He knew every player, held the baseball card of each batter in his hand as they approached the plate, their strong arms pumping two, three bats at a time. The pitcher's card he held in the other hand, and I imagined the statistics stacking up for just a second, and then surrendered the thought to the moment.

There was the chance fly ball towards our bleacher seats, and the automatic roar would follow, the rush to the feet of this huge consciousness I heard when we heaved. I felt the periodic slam of the pulse of this collective crowd. The emotional flush of a stadium in love, in love with the game for being just that, a game. Not a result, not a number, not the risk or the thrill, not the money, nothing but just the excitement of the game.

And there was a screen, like the biggest damn television set you could ever imagine set right across from the bleachers in the grandstands. I watched as it panned across the crowd searching among the faces for the one emotion to sum up the moment. It landed on a man holding a small boy.

The man was me, and I was smiling.

At some point during that game, I momentarily broke the surface of this new reality and became lucidly aware of the paths I had come to this point. I felt the eyes of unseen thousands staring at televisions behind closed bar doors, in dens and kitchens, white knuckled, grinning like mad, eyes wild, hearts pounding. Staring from the past behind closed doors in speakeasies, in houses of ill repute.

But that thrill seemed gone for me now, for it appeared as a filtered emotion, this excitement, run through society's need for this security and the animal urge for risk and for danger.

Far purer than that was the shine I saw in the boy's eyes when that stray ball sailed into the stands, the energy as he lifted his glove, miles away from the brown stitching of the ball. Far better was feeling alive, feeling free for the first time in forever.

Far better was attending my first baseball game and viewing the reality behind the statistics that I'd given my whole life to.

Baseball's never been a kid's game, at least it isn't anymore. But god, I wish it was.

You strip away the uniform and the stands, and you twist the scores, the averages—the numbers—with some strange mathematics and you begin to forget that baseball was supposed to be fun, not just the damn game, but everything, you take the fun from life itself.

The more numbers you have the better you are, the whole world seemed to whisper to me. And for a while, for seventy years, I found myself believing that lie.

But not a moment longer.

You hear what I'm saying? You strip away the magic and in the end, nobody wins.

Throwing Overhand

SHARON HOUCK ROSS

Heather enters dressed for office work. She approaches the dugout, looks in, waves. Pulls out a Polaroid camera and positions herself for a good shot.

HEATHER: Come on out of that dugout and let me take your picture. Put your baseball cap on and come out grinning. I hope you're dirty. Are you good and dirty? Reach down and get some of that dirt. Smear it across your face like this, okay? We'll send the copy to Grandma Rose and write on the back, "KIM, AFTER HITTING THE BALL."

Come on. I'm waiting. Mommie's waiting. Kim?

Okay. I know you're mad. You have a right to be mad. I promised. I tried. But the old man decided to work late. That's the way old men are. Especially old lawyers. Dictating in person instead of using a machine like everybody else. Fussing forever with this clause, dithering around with that one. Senile and stinky. Standing behind you and breathing right into your hair the whole time. Old men lawyers are the worst on their secretaries. I hate him. That's not a nice thing to say, Kimmie, but I do. I truly truly hate and despise him. I should've been at your game. It's Saturday, after all. He said only the morning. But he signs the check that pays the mortgage on our trailer.

I wish I could've seen it. Joey's mom called me when you wouldn't ride home with her. She told me how you hit that ball—thwack! Good for you! It doesn't matter how far it rolled or which direction. You hit the thing, right? This is a first and I'm proud of you. No girl in my family has ever played ball. Come out so I can take your picture.

You might as well get used to it, you know. I intend to take a picture of every triumph in your life. Perfect attendance, student council, debate club, graduation—B.S., M.B.A., Ph.D.—as many graduations as you need. You're gonna get whatever it takes to be the boss. You understand me? So when your kids are counting on you to be somewhere, you can damn well be there.

And that, my dear, is why you are learning to play baseball. Like it or not. It is a game that was never taught to me or my mother. Life is not Vacation Barbie, purple dinosaurs that sing, or baby dolls that wet their britches. So stop wishing for those things. And stop sneaking over to Melissa's house to play with them. *(Positioning the camera)*

Oh, that's attractive. Could you hold that for just another second? Got it! Now get that tongue back in your mouth. Do you see me going around sticking out my tongue when things don't go exactly my way? No. And I think you have played your last game of house with Melissa.

Does Melissa know how to play hardball? Can she stare someone dead in the eye and without blinking, throw them a curve? Is Melissa sneaky enough to steal bases, huh? Is she? Can she run fast, slide through dirt toward a goal and field whatever they hit at her? Hell—can Melissa even throw *overhand*? No. And neither can I. But you are learning. And that's what counts. *(She looks at the developed photograph)*

And the question is, Who are you? Are you this? *(Giving her the photo)* Or are you a winner? Winners look straight into the jaws of disappointment or . . . embarrassment, and they . . . they, well, they put on their cap, come out dirty, and grin big for the camera.

I'm ready. The camera is focused on you. What do you say? *(She waits a full beat. No movement. She sighs and begins to lower the camera. Then she stops, smiles)*

Thatta girl. *(She takes the picture)*

Biographies

LEE BLESSING. The 1992–93 season of the Signature Theatre was devoted to Lee Blessing's work, and included the world premiere of his play *Patient A*. His play *A Walk in the Woods* ran on Broadway, and was subsequently produced in London's West End and Moscow. It has been produced widely in this country and others, and was seen on PBS's American Playhouse. Blessing's plays have premiered at the Manhattan Theatre Club, Yale Repertory Theatre, and La Jolla Playhouse among others, and have won numerous awards. He has twice received grants from the NEA, as well as grants from the Guggenheim, Bush, McKnight, and Jerome Foundations. Heinemann has published two collections of his plays. Blessing's TNT film *Cooperstown*, starring Alan Arkin and Graham Greene, won the Humanitas Prize as well as three nominations for Cable Ace Awards, including best screenplay.

WILMA "WILLIE" BRIGGS played for the Fort Wayne Daisies. Batted second and played right field. A team player whose job was to move the runner along. Played from 1948–1954. Officer of the Players' Association. Hometown: East Greenwich, Rhode Island.

CYNTHIA L. COOPER'S plays have been produced in various venues across the United States and in Canada. Among the theatres in which her work has appeared are The Women's Project and Productions, Primary Stages, Art and Work Ensemble, Wings Theatre, American Renaissance Theatre, Theatreworks USA, West Coast Playwrights, Women's Theatre Collective, Up and Away, Barnard College, Belladonna Theatre, A Daring Theatre, and others. Her plays have won awards from the Hutchinson Festival of New Plays, Double Image, Barn Theatre, POW Festival, and others. For two years, she enjoyed a Jerome Fellowship at the Playwrights Center in Minneapolis, and makes her home in New York City.

GAY DAVIDSON-ZIELSKE. Gay writes and teaches composition, screenwriting, and creative writing at the University of Wisconsin–

Whitewater, and raises her son, Alexander, in Madison. Born Norma Gay Prewett in the Ozarks to industrious parents, she moved with her family to Illinois, where she passed a moody childhood and was eventually dragged kicking and screaming to attend Northern Illinois University. Luckily, she discovered literature there and has been producing it ever since in the form of poems, short stories, reviews, and dramatic writing. Recent work can be found in *For She Is the Tree of Life* (Conari Press), a collection of writings about grandmothers, and *Straight from the Heart* (Lonesome Traveller), an anthology of love poems for which she served as co-editor and contributor.

MERRY ELLEFSON received her M.A. in English/drama from the University of Minnesota and moved to Alaska in 1988. She works as development director/writer for Perseverance Theatre and is currently working on a new play, *Lost in Kubla Khan*.

JEFFERY SCOTT ELWELL is director of theatre and a professor at Mississippi State University. He received his Ph.D. from Southern Illinois University on 1985. He has received a Mississippi Arts Commission Playwriting Fellowship, a Tennessee Williams Scholarship, and an NEH Summer Seminar Fellowship. A member of the Dramatists Guild, his plays have been produced by professional theatres in Chicago, Los Angeles, Memphis, New Orleans, New York, and Roanoke, Virginia. He is currently the chair for the playwrights program for the Association for Theatre in Higher Education, chair of the Southeastern Theatre Conference New Play Project, and PAC chair for ACTF Region IV. He has edited two collections of plays and is currently editing another collection of short plays. In the last year, six of his plays have received productions on Theatre Row in New York and three short plays ran for several months in Los Angeles. Two of those plays, *Escape from Bondage* and *Being Frank*, have been published by Palmetto Play Service. A third play, *The Art of Dating*, was a winner in the Off-Off-Broadway Original Short Play Festival and is being published by Samuel French.

STEVE FEFFER's plays include *Marilyn & Marc*, *The Wizards of Quiz* (published by Dramatists Play Service), *The Mystery Catcher*, and *Bart the Temp: A Story of Wall Street*. His work has been produced or developed at the O'Neill National Playwrights Conference, Ensemble Studio Theatre, Philadelphia Festival Theatre for New Plays, Victory Gardens Theatre, and The National Jewish Theatre. Steve lives and dies each day with his beloved Chicago White Sox.

JUDY GEBAUER's produced plays include *Reclaimed* (Long Wharf Theatre, recipient of the Steinberg Playwriting Award for Excellence); *Bobby Sands, M.P.* (Philadelphia Festival Theatre and the Irish Arts Center, winner of the HBO Writers Award and the Dennis McIntyre Playwriting Award); and *The Hidden Ones* (Philadelphia Festival Theatre, winner of the W. Alton Jones Foundation Grant). *Beer Money*, her one-act Valentine to baseball, was presented at the Bay Area Playwrights Festival. Her one-act, *The Nip and the Bite,* is published in the anthology *Facing Forward.* She has taught basic and experimental playwriting at the University of Iowa and the University of Colorado at Boulder. She was guest lecturer in the University of Iowa's pilot program in Irish studies. She is director of the young playwrights program at the Denver Center Theatre Company, where she received a commission for an original play. She is an associate in the Rocky Mountain Women's Institute and a 1995 recipient of the Colorado Federation of the Arts Innovation Award.

A. BARTLETT GIAMATTI was born in Boston in 1938, and died September 1, 1989. He succeeded Peter Ueberroth as Commissioner of Baseball in April 1989, and from 1986–1989, he had served as president of the National League. A lifelong baseball fan, his selection as commissioner was nevertheless considered unlikely, as he was also a noted medieval and Renaissance scholar (*The Earthly Paradise and the Renaissance Epic; The Play of the Double Senses: Spenser's Fairie Queene*), and taught English and comparative literature at Yale from 1966–1978. He served as Yale's president from 1978–86.

RICHARD HOLODY is an assistant professor of social work at Lehman College, Bronx, New York, and author of *Heather's Babies,* a full-length play about social services in the inner city. He is also a lifelong Cleveland Indians fan and proud owner of a first edition of *The Baseball Encyclopedia.*

MARGARET HUNT has written eight full-length plays, including *Down at Johnnie D's*, which was produced in 1995 on Theatre Row in New York City. She is a recipient of a 1994 playwright's fellowship from the Berrilla Kerr Foundation and two playwright's residencies from the Edward Albee Foundation. She is a member of The Women's Project and Productions, Circle Rep Playwrights Lab, the BMI Librettists Workshop, and the Dramatists Guild.

ROBERT INGHAM grew up on a farm in Virginia. His father recited Shakespeare to pass the time in the fields and his mother was an insatiable storyteller. He took a degree in history from the University of Virginia and studied playwriting with John Gassner at the Yale Scool of Drama. He taught at Grinnell College, the University of Montana, the University of Virginia, and Mary Washington College; acted with the Long Wharf Theatre, the Milwaukee Repertory Theater, and the Goodman Theatre, among others; and wrote *A Simple Life, No Better,* and *Custer* as well as television scripts and short stories. Robert Ingham died in 1992.

SUSAN E. JOHNSON was born and raised in Rockford, Illinois, where she was a girlhood fan of the Rockford Peaches. She has her Ph.D. in sociology and has taught at numerous colleges and universities around the country. Presently, Susan lives in Anchorage, Alaska, where she is a consultant to students and organizations in research design as well as a writer. She is a member of the All-American Girls Professional Baseball League Players' Association, the Society for American Baseball Research, and The Women's Sports Foundation.

ARTHUR KOPIT is the author of *Oh Dad, Poor Dad, Mamma's Hung You in the Closet and I'm Feelin' So Sad* (Vernon Rice Award, Outer Circle Award), *Indians* (Tony Nominee), *Wings* (Tony Nominee, Prix Italia for radio version of play), the book for the musical *Nine* (Tony Award for Best Musical, 1982*), End of the World with Symposium to Follow,* a new translation of Ibsen's *Ghosts, Road to Nirvana,* and the book for the musical *Phantom,* based on Gaston Leroux's *The Phantom of the Opera* (music and lyrics by Maury Yeston). *Phantom,* written prior to the Lloyd Webber version, is currently playing in theaters around the country, and has been on tour in Germany and Scandinavia for the past three years. Also, various one-act plays, including *Chamber Music, The Day the Whores Came Out to Play Tennis, Conquest of Everest, The Questioning of Nick, The Hero, Success,* and *Good Help Is Hard to Find.* TV films include the NBC miniseries *Hands of a Stranger,* the NBC miniseries of his *Phantom of the Opera,* the CBS miniseries *In a Child's Name,* and most recently, *Roswell.* He is currently at work on a new play, *Mrs. Gaskell and the Doomsday Machine.* He is also at work on a musical based on the film *Sweet Smell of Success,* to be produced by Garth Drabinsky, with music by Cy Coleman and lyrics by Susan Birkenhead; a musical based on Philip Barry's *The Philadelphia Story,* using the music of Cole Porter; and an original musical called *Eureka!* with music and lyrics by Maury Yeston. Mr. Kopit is the recipient of numerous awards, including Shaw Traveling fellow, Harvard 1959; Guggenheim fellow 1967; Rockefeller grantee 1968; Award for Literature, American Institute of Arts and Letters, 1971; N.E.H. grantee 1974; fellow, Center for Humanities, Wesleyan University 1974–75, playwright-in-residence 1975–76; CBS fellow Yale University 1976–77, adjunct professor of playwriting, Yale School of Drama, 1977–80; adjunct professor of playrwriting, CCNY 1981–1994. He is a member of the Dramatists Guild, the Dramatists Guild Council, Writers Guild of America, and PEN. Mr. Kopit is married to the writer Leslie Garis. They live in Connecticut and have three children: Alex, Ben, and Kathleen.

HOWARD KORDER was born in New York City in 1957, and graduated from the State University of New York at Binghamton. His play *Boys' Life* was presented by Lincoln Center in 1988, directed by W. H. Macy and featuring the Atlantic Theatre Company, and received a nomination for a Pulitzer Prize. It is produced frequently at theatres here and around the world. Other plays include *Night Maneuver* (1982); *The Middle Kingdom* (1985); *Lip Service* (1985), his adaptation of which was broadcast by HBO in 1989, winning cable television's Ace Award for best theatrical presentation; *Episode 26* (1985); *Fun* (1987); *Nobody* (1987); *Search and Destroy* (1990); and *The Lights* (1993). *Search and Destroy* was commissioned by California's South Coast Repertory, premiering there in 1990 under the direction of David Chambers. It received the Los Angeles Theatre Critics' Award for best new play, and the Joseph Kesselring Prize from the National Arts Club. A production at Yale Repertory

Theatre followed, and the play opened on Broadway at Circle in the Square in 1992. A critically acclaimed production of *Search and Destroy* opened at the Royal Court Theatre in London in May 1993 under the direction of Stephen Daldry. Korder's play *The Lights* was produced at Lincoln Center Theatre in fall 1993 under the direction of Mark Wing-Davey and received seven Drama Desk nominations and an Obie Award for Playwriting. Korder wrote the screenplay adaptation of *Boys' Life* for Scott Rudin. He then wrote *Love and Bullets*, an original screenplay for producer Art Linson at Warner Brothers. He has written for Errol Morris, director of *The Thin Blue Line* and *A Brief History of Time*, and his most recent feature assignment was *The Passion of Ayn Rand* for Showtime. In television, Korder was story editor of the hit CBS series *Kate and Allie*. He has written a number of half-hour pilots, among them *Bright Ideas* (for Scholastic Productions and Universal Television) and *Mister Normal* and *Bark!* for Viacom; and an hour pilot called *The Institute* (co-written with David Yazbek for the Arthur Company). *Boys' Life, Fun* and *Nobody, Search and Destroy, The Lights, Night Maneuver* and *The Pope's Nose* (a collection of short plays) are available in published form from Dramatists Play Service. *The Middle Kingdom, Lip Service,* and *Episode 26* are published by Samuel French. *Boys' Life, Fun* and *Nobody, The Middle Kingdom, Lip Service,* and *Search and Destroy* are also available from Grove Press.

GAIL KRIEGEL wrote *The Whites of Their Eyes*, a screenplay optioned by SS Films; the book and lyrics for *Reverend Jenkins & His Almost All Colored Orphanage Band*, with music by Luther Henderson, and *Rainbow Junction*, a WCBS-TV Christmas Special. Her plays *On The Home Front* and *Holy Places* have been produced in various regional theatres and in New York, Los Angeles, and Chicago. For her work, she has received a Rockefeller Foundation fellowship, the Ruby Lloyd Apsey Award for Playwriting, and the National Playwriting Award for Children's Theatre. Gail is a member of the Dramatists Guild, BMI Librettists & Lyricists Workshop, The Women's Project and Productions, and PEN. Presently, she is finishing a novel and starting on the book and lyrics for a new musical.

In 1981, KEN LAZEBNIK founded *The Minneapolis Review of Baseball* (now *The Elysian Fields Quarterly*), a literary quarterly focused on baseball. Along with its current editor Steve Lehman, he wrote a children's baseball book, *A Is for At Bat*, and edited an anthology of writing from the magazine *Base Paths*. He's written baseball pieces for *The New York Times* and *Manhattan Inc.* Since 1989, he's been a contributing writer to Garrison Keillor's *A Prairie Home Companion*. His work as a playwright includes the one-man show *Calvinisms* and, most recently, rewriting the book for the Guthrie Theatre production of *Babes in Arms*. He has written for such television programs as *Jack's Place*, *The Paula Poundstone Show*, and *Touched by an Angel*, where he is a story editor.

TOM LINKLATER was born and raised in Oregon and moved to Alaska in 1975. He works part-time for Perseverance Theatre and is currently finishing up a play about teen violence entitled *Fire with Fire*.

HEATHER MCDONALD's new play, *An Almost Holy Picture*, premiered at the La Jolla Playhouse and was named best new play of the year by the L.A. Times Critics Association. Her other plays are *Dream of a Common Language*, *The Rivers and Ravines*, *Available Light*, and *Faulkner's Bicycle*, produced at Berkeley Repertory Theatre, Arena Stage, The Actors Theatre of Louisville, Yale Repertory Theatre, and Theatre of the First Amendment. She's twice been awarded NEA playwriting fellowships. She lives in Washington, D.C., with her husband, Bennett Minton, and daughters, Louise and Marilyn Grace.

CYNTHIA MERCATI is the author of over twenty published plays, as well as numerous articles, essays, and short stories. She is also a professional actress and a current member of Actors on Tour, the professional children's theatre from the Des Moines Playhouse, who take shows—among them, several of her own scripts—to schools, libraries, and communities all over Iowa. She is also on the roster of Iowa Artists in the Schools and Communities, the owner of a rotund dachshund, and a baseball fanatic—the Chicago White Sox being her main men!

JAMES R. MILLER was born in Salt Lake City, raised in the Midwest, and began writing and acting solo pieces for competition and for local Illinois community theatres while still in high school. After four years service in the Marine Corps as both a combat journalist and satellite specialist, he began publishing articles in local newspapers and international magazines. Twenty-four years old, he resides in DeKalb, Illinois, where he owns a successful fitness business.

LILLIAN MORRISON is the author of several books of poems, among them *The Sidewalk Racer* and *The Break Dance Kids*, both of which deal with sports. She has also compiled four poetry anthologies on sports and rhythm, most recently *At the Crack of a Bat* (baseball poems) and *Slam Dunk* (basketball poems), both published by Hyperion. Her work has appeared in numerous magazines and anthologies.

LAVONNE MUELLER's play *Letters to a Daughter from Prison*, about Nehru and his daughter, Indira, was produced at the First International Festival of the Arts in New York City, and went on to tour in India. Her play *Violent Peace* was produced in London in 1992 and was the Critics Choice in *Time Out Magazine*. Her play *Little Victories* was produced in Tokyo by Theatre Classic Productions and directed by Riho Mitachi. *The Only Woman General* was produced in New York City and went on to the Edinburgh Festival where it was Pick of the Fringe by the Scottish critics. She was awarded the Roger Stevens Playwriting Award, which she received at the Kennedy Center in Washington, D.C., in 1992. She is a Woodrow Wilson scholar, and a Lila Wallace Reader's Digest writing fellow, and has received a Guggenheim grant, a Rockefeller grant, three National Endowment for the Arts grants, a Fulbright to Argentina, an Asian Culture Council grant to Calcutta, India, and a USA Friendship Commission grant to Japan. Her plays have been published by Dramatists Play Service, Samuel French, Applause Books, Performing Arts Journal, Theatre Communication Group, Heinemann, and Baker's Plays. Her textbook, *Creative Writing,* published by Doubleday and the National Textbook Company, is used by students around the world. She has taught at the University of Iowa and at Columbia University. As a Woodrow Wilson visiting scholar, she has helped colleges around the United States set up writing programs. She has been an Arts America speaker for USIS (United States Information Service) in India, Finland, Romania, Japan, Yugoslavia, and Norway. She was recently a

Fulbright fellow to Jordan and recently received a National Endowment for the Humanities grant to do research in Paris.

ANDRÉA J. ONSTAD is a writer and artist. She lives in Kentfield, California, with her husband and teaches at the University of San Francisco and the College of Marin.

JOAN PUMA, a native Texan and former "Night Life" reporter for *The New Yorker* for over thirteen years, has had fiction and essays published in *Tumblewords: Writers Reading the West* (1995, University of Nevada Press), *Weber Studies, Wigwag, The New York Times,* and *Grand Street. Spit!* was produced in 1989 by the University of Virginia Department of Drama. Puma, a member of the Dramatists Guild, lives in Wyoming.

RICHARD STOCKTON RAND has had dramatic work published in *Sycamore Review, Hopewell Review: New Work by Indiana's Best Writers, Hyphen, Slipstream,* and *Indiana Theatre Review.* As a solo performer of original work, he has toured his one-person shows, *little guys, i dreamed i was a baseball card, and A History of Comedy,* to over one hundred theatres and universities throughout the United States, Canada, and Europe. *i dreamed i was a baseball card* received critical acclaim at the Fringe Festival of Toronto in 1995 and was voted a top-ten show at the Winnipeg Fringe by CBC TV and Radio. Currently, he is an associate professor of theatre at Purdue University. Prior to his academic career, he acted on Broadway, Off-Broadway, and at numerous regional theatres.

KENNETH ROBBINS is originally from Bill Arp, Georgia, received his M.F.A. from the University of Georgia, and his Ph.D. from Southern Illinois University–Carbondale. He has been a professor of theatre at the University of South Dakota for the past ten years. His first novel, *Buttermilk Bottoms,* received the 1986 Toni Morrison Prize and the Associated Writing Programs Novel Award. As a playwright, his works for the stage have been produced by the New Works Theatre, the World Premiere Theatre, Dallas Theatre Center, the Nashville Academy Theatre, Theatre Atlanta Off Peachtree, and the Project Arts Center, Dublin, Ireland. Among his works for the stage are *Atomic Field,* winner of the SETC New Play Award, *The Coke Machine Kids,* recipient of the Festival of

Southern Theatre Award, *Molly's Rock*, Literary Achievement Award from the New Works Theatre, and *The Hunger Feast*, published by Palmetto Play Service. Presently, Dr. Robbins lives in Vermillion, South Dakota, with his wife and two children.

SHARON HOUCK ROSS is playwright-in-residence and literary manager for The Women's Project and Productions in New York, where she teaches the Playwrights Lab. Her plays include *Trapped Daylight* (produced by New Georges), *11 Shades of White: The Story of Veronica Lake* (at The Women's Project and The Open Stage Theatre in Pittsburgh), *Game!* (Circle Rep Lab), and *Entry Points* (Iowa Festival of New Plays). Sharon is a 1993 M.F.A. graduate from the Iowa Playwrights Workshop at the University of Iowa.

KATE MOIRA RYAN is a member of New Dramatists. In 1994 her play *The Autobiography of Aiken Fiction* was produced in New York by The Women's Project. She has written a musical with composer Kim Sherman about the Irish immigrant experience entitled *Leaving Queens*, which was workshopped in the spring of 1996. *100 Strikes* is from a full-length untitled piece that has yet to be written.

ELEANORE C. SPEERT is the author of *Peripheral Vision*, which was produced in New York by I.C.A.N.I. productions. Her play *Quartet Nights, or the Last Good Time We Had* was published by Penguin Books in the anthology *Moving Parts*. She has had sponsored staged readings of her plays, including *Rhumbold, Dear Anna, Something So Simple*, and many others. She has worked with The Character Company as a writer for the Manhattan Punchline's comedy revue team, The Punchline Players. She is the publications director at Dramatists Play Service, Inc.

ALAN THURSTON is an actor/playwright who resides in New York City. *Shoeless Joe*, his first play, was a Eugene O'Neill Playwrights Conference finalist and was produced by the Chicago Actors Ensemble. He received a Certificate for Playwriting Achievement for his work on the play from the International Society of Dramatists. Alan is a member of the Dramatists Guild and Actors Equity Association.

THOMAS G. WAITES received his M.F.A. in playwriting from the University of Iowa. He has directed both regional and off-

Broadway theatre. He wrote and directed *Prayer in a Bar* at the Actors Studio in New York, and *Blue Moon*, which was produced to critical acclaim in Los Angeles. He has appeared as an actor on and off Broadway with Al Pacino, Judith Ivey, and Johnny Pankow. He is also the author of the one-man play *Dark Laughter*.